T0114910

Why Is God Calling All Jews Back to Their Homeland?

by James W. Tygrett

WESTBOW
P R E S S®
A DIVISION OF THOMAS NELSON
& ZONDERVAN

WestBow Press books may be ordered through booksellers or by contacting:

WestBow Press
A Division of Thomas Nelson & Zondervan
1663 Liberty Drive
Bloomington, IN 47403
www.westbowpress.com
844-714-3454

ISBN: 979-8-3850-1332-6 (sc)
ISBN: 979-8-3850-1333-3 (e)

Library of Congress Control Number: 2023922539

Print information available on the last page.

WestBow Press rev. date: 12/13/2023

Hear, O Israel: The Lord our God, the Lord is one! You shall love the Lord your God with all your heart, with all your soul, and with all your strength." Deuteronomy 6:4-5

Contents

Introduction

This book is about Jews, as the title suggests, and for Jews. Others may enjoy knowing what God has planned for Jews in the near and distant future.

The first chapter is about God calling. The first Jew was Abram, the man God called to leave his home and family. God wanted him to leave his family who worshiped idols and separate by moving to a new land. Abram worshiped God in the land of Canaan. We will look at the reasons Abram's faith was tested. He sets a good example for us today.

Then we will look at how and why God called Moses. God not only had prepared him for the call but He had sent an assistant to work with him. Moses' faith in God's call set his heart to be fully committed to obeying God. Moses was tested along the journey of leading the nation of Israel through the wilderness. He wrote down prophecies about the future of Abraham's descendants. Some of the prophecies will be included in this writing. God's call to each Jew was given at Mount Sinai.

The calling of two judges—Gideon and Samuel—will be studied. Why and how God called them will reveal the reasons they were called which includes their faith and obedience to God's covenant. Each was God's judge for his generation.

The kingdom of Israel is reviewed in chapter two. The kings of the twelve tribes are studied regarding their commitment to God's covenant. We will see the reason the ten northern tribes rebelled and established a separate nation, the kingdom of Israel. Some of the prophets' warnings to Israel will be reviewed to help us understand God's anger against them. We will see the reason their kingdom was destroyed and many taken into captivity.

The third chapter addresses Judah, the kingdom of the southern tribes. As each king is reviewed, we will see how God viewed their commitment to His covenant. We will see the reason some were blessed and others were judged. The reason the kingdom was destroyed and many taken into captivity will be reviewed.

Prophecies referring to the latter days will be studied in the fourth chapter. This will help us understand the timing of the Jews' returning the "second time" to their homeland. It may give us the season when Gog from the land of Magog will come against the nation of Israel.

The prophecies of Daniel are studied in chapter five. The dream of chapter 2 is placed in Table 2 with the visions of chapters 7, 8, 9, 11, and 12 to help us understand the relationships between them. These prophecies give us the Gentile kingdoms that will rule the world until the Messiah comes and sets up His kingdom in Jerusalem.

Chapter 9 of Daniel gives us two time periods of Gentile governments. The first period was completed when Jerusalem was destroyed in AD 70. The second period is still future, and the details will be studied in this chapter of this book.

Questions are answered in the sixth chapter of this book. You will find the answer to the title of this book in chapter 6.

God is still calling today for each Jew to accept Him as Lord and to answer His call to come home.

1

God's Call

Abram

> Now the LORD had said to Abram: "Get out of your country, from your family and from your father's house, to a land that I will show you." (Genesis 12:1)

The God who made the universe and everything on this earth spoke to Abram: "I am Almighty God; walk before Me and be blameless" (Genesis 17:1). Abram knew it was Almighty God because no one can duplicate God's holy and powerful presence. Abram was worshipping God when others were worshipping idols.

The relationship between God and Abram was not like the relationship God had with Adam. God had made Adam from the dust of the earth to worship Him of his own free will. God made the best garden ever and placed His creation in that beautiful garden. Adam was made in the likeness of God. God loved Adam and proved it by the beautiful garden He made. God did not leave Adam but had fellowship with him. God came down in the cool of the day (Genesis 3:8) to walk in fellowship with Adam whom He loved. Adam and Eve were familiar with the sound of God walking in the Garden of Eden.

God's message for Abram was clear: Abram was to leave where he was living in Haran. It seems clear that God wanted Abram to separate himself from idol worship and follow God. It also included leaving his family who had moved earlier from Ur of the Chaldeans to Haran. The family of Terah, Abram's father, more than likely followed the Euphrates River up to Haran. This move may have made it easier for Abram to leave his second home than it would have been to leave the land of his birth.

By no means was God's message to Abram without a specific destination in mind, but the location was not given to Abram. God did not give Abram a map or written instructions. It took faith for Abram to believe God would tell him when he had arrived. For Abram to move out from Haran, he had to have faith in God's instructions. It is clear that Abram did step out in faith and obeyed the Lord because of His love.

God was calling Abram to be separate from the culture of idolatry and to serve God personally. He was able to have an individual, loving relationship with God on a daily basis. That does not mean God visited him every day, but Abram lived as if God was with him every day.

This obedience by Abram, because of his faith in God, made his relationship with God personal and fulfilling. This is true for all those who will humble themselves and put their trust and faith in the creator of the universe today.

"I will make you a great nation; I will bless you and make your name great; and you shall be a blessing." (Genesis 12:2)

God has recorded His faithfulness to Abram (Abraham[1]) and his descendants through Isaac, those who put their faith in God's promises. All through the Holy Scriptures, Abraham's faith is remembered.

"I will bless those who bless you, and I will curse him who curses you; and in you all the families of the earth shall be blessed." (Genesis 12:3)

Abram was seventy-five years old when he left Haran in obedience to God's call. Lot, his nephew, went with him as

---

1 "No longer shall your name be called Abram, but your name shall be Abraham; for I have made you a father of many nations." (Genesis 17:5)

well as all the people he had hired to care for his livestock. This made a large group of people that moved with Abram.

God selected Abram because of his faith and obedience to God. He promised Abram that from his family would come the Messiah Redeemer for all people of the earth. This would be fulfilled through the son of promise—Isaac.

Abram traveled through Shechem into the land of the Canaanites. Then God told Abram, "To your descendants I will give this land" (Genesis 12:7). Abram had arrived in the land to which God had called him.

Abram and his nephew Lot had large numbers of animals, and their herdsmen came into conflict over the pastureland. To end the strife, Abram gave Lot the first choice of land to claim for his family. Abraham would live separately, on other land. Lot chose the plains of the Jordan. After he separated from Abram, the Lord said to Abram, "Lift your eyes now and look from the place where you are—northward, southward, eastward, and westward; for all the land which you see I give to you and your descendants forever. And I will make your descendants as the dust of the earth, so that if a man could number the dust of the earth, then your descendants also could be numbered" (Genesis 13:14–16).

God promised to give Abram's descendants the land he was in. This is coming true in our day because He has brought many Jews back to their homeland since the Second World War. The nation of Israel was birthed on May 14, 1948. The "forever" will be fulfilled when the Messiah comes to rule the world.

The Lord said to Abram, "Do not be afraid, Abram, I am your shield, your exceedingly great reward" (Genesis 15:1). When Abram told the Lord he had no heir except Eliezer of Damascus, his manager, the Lord replied, "This one shall not be your heir, but one who will come from your own body shall be your heir" (Genesis 15:4).Then the Lord led Abram outside and showed him the stars of heaven. He told Abram that his descendants would be as numerous as the stars he saw in the heavens. "And he believed in the LORD, and He accounted it to him for righteousness" (Genesis 15:6).

Note that God took Abram's *belief,* or faith, in the *Lord's promises* and counted it as Abram's *righteousness.* The same is true today. When a Jew believes in the promises of the Lord with all his or her heart, the desire to obey the Lord's instructions as Abram did follows naturally. There is no other way for a personal relationship with God. Faith must come first in believing the promises of God who created the universe; obedience to His instructions must follow.

The Lord instructed Abram to bring an offering of a three-year-old heifer, a three-year-old female goat, a three-year-old ram, a turtledove, and a young pigeon. After Abram prepared the offerings, God told him that his descendants would serve in a strange land for four hundred years because the Amorites' iniquity was not yet full or complete. Then Abram's descendants would return to this land. When the Amorites were full of iniquity, God would bring the children of Abram, through Isaac, back to this land. Israel would drive out and replace the Amorites. It seems that God has a limit to the iniquity He will tolerate in a nation.

God made a covenant with Abram that his descendants would be given the land between the river of Egypt and the Euphrates River. This will happen when the Messiah sets up His kingdom on earth. This may be closer than many people think. The timing is reviewed later in this book.

The covenant God made with Abram is affirmed in Genesis 17. In the covenant, God changed Abram's name to Abraham because he would become a father to many nations. He changed Sarai's name to Sarah. The covenant extended only to Abraham's descendants through the promised son, Isaac. Abraham accepted the Lord's covenant by circumcising each male in his household as an act of worship. Again, Abraham was obedient to God's instruction because he believed His promises by faith.

"And I will establish My covenant between Me
and you and your descendants after you in their
generations, for an everlasting covenant, to be God to
you and your descendants after you." (Genesis 17:7)
This everlasting covenant was for each generation that
followed Abraham. Each generation had to put their faith in
God's promises just as had Abraham. Their faith had to be
from their heart, soul, and strength. Each generation needed
to be taught but they had to accept God's promises from their
heart and follow God's instructions. We will see that God made
a covenant with the people of Israel when they came out of
Egypt. Each generation had to believe God's promises by faith
and live by His instructions.

After Abraham was circumcised in obedience, God
gave him the promise of a son the following year. This is
worth noting because God has not changed and still requires
obedience by faith from each individual Jew, male or female.

In Genesis 18, Abraham meets the Lord and two angels
who look like young men. He feeds them and the Lord. The
Lord makes a promise to Abraham. "I (the Lord) will certainty
return to you according to the time of life, and behold, Sarah
your wife shall have a son." (Sarah was listening in the tent
door which was behind him.) Now Abraham and Sarah were
old, well advanced in age; and Sarah had passed the age of
childbearing" (Genesis 18:10–11).

The Lord allowed Abraham to intercede for the cities of
Sodom and Gomorrah. The Lord was sending the angels to
Sodom to see if the iniquity in the cities needed to be dealt with
because the outcry against the wicked cities was great.

The Lord visited Sarah as He had promised. Sarah
conceived and bore Abraham a son in his old age at the time
God had set. Abraham called his son who was born to him—
whom Sarah bore to him—Isaac. Abraham circumcised his son
Isaac when he was eight days old, as God had commanded him
(Genesis 21:1–4).

Abraham had obeyed God by moving and trusting that God would give him a son. Now, after twenty-five years of trusting and serving God, Abraham was blessed with the son God had promised him. Scripture does not say God loved Abraham but it does show us that God loved him.

Sarah saw Ishmael[2], the son of Hagar, her maidservant, mocking Isaac. She strongly requested that Abraham send Hagar and her son away so he would not inherit anything that belonged to Isaac, the promised son from God. When Abraham talked to God about it, God said: "Do not let it be displeasing in your sight because of the Lad or because of your bondwoman. Whatever Sarah has said to you, listen to her voice; for in Isaac your seed shall be called." (Genesis 21:12)

Through Isaac's descendants the Messiah would come. The word "seed" is not plural because it is referring to the Messiah who will bless the families of the world. This separates all the other children Abraham had from the promised son, Isaac.

There is a principle in this verse that should be considered. The son of the bondwoman was not to receive any part of the promised son of the free woman's life or inheritance. The descendants of Abraham through Isaac were to be free by their faith in God to serve the Lord through obeying His instructions, as had Abraham and Sarah before them.

The son of the bondwoman represents the self-centered and arrogant life that refuses to humble itself before an Almighty God. God has a righteous standard for His believers to live by to be acceptable to Him. It all begins by believing in all the promises of God as Abraham demonstrated. Abraham's faith was then followed by obedience to all of God's instructions.

God tested Abraham's faith again in Genesis 22. "Now it came to pass after these things that God tested Abraham, and said to him, 'Abraham!' And he said, 'Here I am.' Then He said, 'Take now your son, your only son Isaac, whom you love,

---

2 Ishmael, fourteen years old at this time, was a son of Abraham by Hagar, the maidservant Sarai had shared with her husband when she, herself, had no son. Genesis 16.

and go to the land of Moriah, and offer him there as a burnt offering on one of the mountains of which I shall tell you.'" (vv. 1–2)

Abraham did not ask, "Why?" or " Are You sure, God?" The next morning, he set out with some young men of his household. When he saw the mountain, he told the young men to stay with their supplies. "Stay here with the donkey; the lad and I will go yonder and worship, and *we* will come back to you" (v. 22:5, emphasis added by author).

Abraham's faith in God's word was so firm that he believed, when he sacrificed Isaac, God would raise Isaac from the ashes. That is why he told the young men "*we*" will return.

Abraham prepared the altar and placed Isaac on the altar. When he raised the knife to kill his son, the angel of the Lord stopped him. God had provided a sacrifice—a ram was caught in a thicket behind him.

> "By Myself I have sworn, says the LORD, because you have done this thing, and have not withheld your son, your only son—blessing I will bless you, and multiplying I will multiply your descendants as the stars of the heaven and as the sand which is on the seashore; and your descendants shall possess the gate of their enemies. In your seed all the nations of the earth shall be blessed, because you have obeyed My voice." (Genesis 22:16–18)

God's response affirmed His promise to multiply Abraham's descendants through Isaac. The reason for God's promise is recorded: "Because you have obeyed My voice" (v. 18). There is no doubt that Abraham's descendants should obey the voice of God.

Abraham set the pattern for all his descendants to follow— faith in God's promises and obedience to all God's instructions. One can see that God loved Abraham and continues to love the children of Abraham through Isaac because God has *never withdrawn or cancelled His promises.*

"Obey My voice, and I will be your God, and you
shall be My people. And walk in all the ways that I
have commanded you, that it may be well with you."
(Jeremiah 7:23)

These words have been true for every Jew. God's voice
speaks from the holy Scriptures to the one who has faith in
God's promises. Almighty God wants to send His blessings of
love to each Jew who believes in Him and obeys His voice.

Moses

Abraham was told by God that his descendants would live
in a strange land for four hundred years (Genesis 15:13). This
happened when Jacob and his entire family moved to Egypt
because of the famine while Joseph was ruler in Egypt. God
had been with Joseph when he was taken to Egypt. God used
him to prepare for the famine that was coming upon the land.

Moses' parents were of the tribe of Levi. It is fascinating
to read how Pharaoh's daughter found the infant Moses, then
returned him to his own mother and paid her to raise her own
son. When he was old enough, Moses returned to grow up in
the palace, learning the language and all the traditions and
details of Pharaoh's kingdom.

Moses fled Egypt after he had slain an Egyptian in an
attempt to help his brethren. When he realized the murder
had been witnessed, he went to the land Midian. He married
Zipporah, the daughter of Jethro. He cared for his father-in-
law's flock.

One day Moses came to the mountain of Horeb while
leading the flock. He saw a bush which was on fire but was not
burning up.

"I am the God of your father—the God of Abraham,
the God of Isaac, and the God of Jacob. . . . I have
surely seen the oppression of My people who are
in Egypt, and have heard their cry because of their
taskmasters, for I know their sorrows. So I have come

down to deliver them out of the hand of the Egyptians,
and to bring them up from that land to a good and
large land, to a land flowing with milk and honey."
(Exodus 3:6–8)

It was obvious that Moses was talking with God because the
bush did not burn up. God called Moses by name and told him
to take off his sandals because he was standing on holy ground,
the presence of Almighty God.

Moses initially felt he was inadequate to carry out God's
instructions, but God promised to be with him. Next, he wanted
to know what name to use to explain who had sent him. God
said, "I AM WHO I AM" (Exodus 3:14). Moses was not sure
the elders of Israel would believe him so God had him throw
down his rod; it instantly became a snake. He picked up the
snake, and it became a rod again. God had Moses put his hand
in his bosom. When he pulled it out, it had become leprous. He
repeated the motion, and his hand was healthy again.

Then Moses said he was slow of speech and of tongue, so
God said Aaron, his brother, could speak for Moses. Then the
Lord said to Moses, "Go, return to Egypt; for all the men who
sought your life are dead" (Exodus 4:19). This was God's call
for Moses to have faith and obey His instructions.

Moses was faithful to follow God's directions for the next
forty years. He was committed to daily teach each generation
God's instructions.

The Egyptians had made slaves of the Israelites and were
abusing them (Exodus 1:11–14). Fearful of an uprising by the
large number of Israelite slaves, Pharaoh ordered the midwives
to kill all newborn Jewish boys (1:8–22). This action brought
the wrath of God against Egypt. He did much harm in Egypt
through the plagues. The ten plagues God sent against Egypt
are recorded in Exodus 7–11. All ten plagues were judgment
against the gods of Egypt (Exodus 12:12).

Those who put their trust in God, however, did not experience the wrath of God. They saw deliverance. The plague of flies in Egypt did not enter the land of Goshen where the Israelites lived (see Exodus 8:21–22). The plague on the livestock, horses, donkeys, and camels of the Egyptians killed none of the Israelites' animals (Exodus 9:4). The plague of boils affected the Egyptians but not the Jews (Exodus 9:11).

The plague of hail on Egypt did not fall in the land of Goshen (Exodus 9:26). The plague of locusts covered the land of Egypt (Exodus 10:12–19). A plague of darkness that could be felt covered Egypt, but in the land of the Israelites there was light (Exodus 10:23). The last plague was the death of the firstborn of every Egyptian family and beast. But no death touched the Israelites' homes if they had the blood of a lamb applied to the sides and top of the doorframes of their homes. God was showing the children of Israel His blessing and love. (Exodus 12:12–13)

> He cast on them the fierceness of His anger, wrath, indignation, and trouble, by sending angels of destruction among them. He made a path for His anger; He did not spare their soul from death, but gave their life over to the plague, and destroyed all the firstborn in Egypt, the first of their strength in the tents of Ham. But He made His own people go forth like sheep, and guided them in the wilderness like a flock. (Psalm 78:49–52)

One can see why God "made a path for His anger" with judgments and wrath because His holiness required it. Delivering the children of Israel from Egyptian slavery was the love of Almighty God in action. There can be no doubt.

The last event is called the Passover by the Jews because the death angel passed over the Jews' homes that had the blood applied to their doorposts. Each year, in Israel and in many homes around the world, Jews still observe a feast in commemoration of the night the slaves were freed.

God's people, the Israelites, were spared God's wrath which was poured out on the ungodly, the Egyptians. We see the true character of God: He is just and fair. His wrath is held in reserve for those who have no thoughts of Him and have no fear of answering to Him. One can see that God will make a path for His anger to be poured out on ungodly, rebellious, and perverted nations. The nation who experienced the wrath of God at this time was Egypt.

God saw the cruelty of the Egyptians toward the Israelites and the murder of the baby boys, which brought His wrath. The Israelites were delivered from slavery because of God's loving action. God made a nation from the descendants of Abraham, Isaac, and Jacob. "Your name shall no longer be called Jacob, but Israel; for you have struggled with God and with men, and have prevailed" (Genesis 32:28).

Jacob's heart had to be dealt with by God as he was coming back into the land of promise. He had deceived his father to get his brother's blessing (Genesis 27:20–29). Jacob deceived his father-in-law by selective breeding of Jethro's sheep and goats to increase his own flocks (Genesis 30:28–43). But God changed Jacob's heart when He changed his name from Jacob to Israel.

Egypt had oppressed Israel by abusing them as slaves with no thought of answering to God for their treatment of the slaves. The killing of the Jewish baby boys seems to have been the last straw that moved the hand of God. God had prepared a man to lead the Jews out of Egypt: Moses. When God sent Moses back to lead the Jews out of Egypt, Moses knew the customs and the places of the royal kingdom; he knew all aspects of the Egyptian nation and the traditions of the royal family. God had prepared him during the time he had lived in Egypt.

God's Call to Every Jew

In the third month, after the Israelites left Egypt, they came to the wilderness of Sinai and camped at Mount Sinai. The Lord gave a message to Moses for the children of Israel. "You have seen what I did to the Egyptians, and how I bore you on eagles' wings and brought you to Myself. Now therefore, if you will indeed obey My voice and keep My covenant, then you shall be a special treasure to Me above all people; for all the earth is Mine. And you shall be to Me a kingdom of priests and a holy nation" (Exodus 19:4–6).

God's desire was for each Jew to see His deliverance—"I bore you on eagles' wings and brought you to Myself"—as an act of His Love. Then they would put their trust in God and "obey [His] voice and keep [His] covenant." Through obedience, they became a *"special treasure"* to Him. Then God would be able to bless them and pour out His love on them abundantly. They would be "a kingdom of priests and a holy nation" to the Lord.

This generous offer from God was conditional. They had to put their faith in the Lord, worship Him only, and obey His voice. Remember, this offer has never been cancelled or withdrawn. It is still available today for each Jew.

God gave the Ten Commandments to israel from Sinai Mountain (Exodus 20). God's covenant with Abraham now includes spiritual and moral laws.

God's covenant with Israel contributed to their formation. God's plan was for each individual to accept the covenant and have a personal relationship with Him. Then the nation of Israel would be a holy nation before the Lord.

As the Israelites stood before the mountain, Moses spoke with God and God answered from the mount. This is God's call to all Jews of each generation. The quotations are the first phrase of each thought.

"I am the LORD your God."
"You shall have no other gods before Me."
"You shall not make for yourself a carved image."
"You shall not take the name of the LORD your God in vain."
"Remember the Sabbath day, to keep it holy."
"Honor your father and your mother."
"You shall not murder."
"You shall not commit adultery."
"You shall not steal."
"You shall not bear false witness against you neighbor."
"You shall not covet . . . anything that is your neighbor's."
(Exodus 20:2–17)

The people trembled and shook with fear. They asked Moses to talk with God and let them know what He said. Moses replied, "Do not fear; for God has come to test you, and that His fear may be before you, so that you may not sin" (Exodus 20:20). Moses had a reverential fear of God while the people's fear came from a lack of reverence for God.

The people saw God with fleshly hearts, not a heart of faith like that of Jacob who wrestled with God and would not let go until God blessed him. Jacob's experience was not a one-time decision but a continuous walk in faith and obedience.

The people's conscience was convicting them. God wanted them to know His covenant would be sufficient to meet His holy standard for them. This was why God spoke aloud so they could experience His holy presence. They would have a reverent fear of God's holiness.

Why was God testing them? First, there should have been no doubt that God existed because they had heard His voice and seen the results of His presence. The Israelites needed to know that Almighty God cared about His creation and wanted them to be His holy people.

Second, God had delivered them from the slavery of Egypt because He loved them and because of His promise to their father Abraham. This should have caused them to believe He would keep all His promises. Their faith should have been strengthened with all the testing God gave them in the wilderness. But their lack of faith was evident in their response to God's testing. Their response was to accuse Moses of bringing them into the wilderness to die.

Third, there is a spiritual and moral standard for people who are called to be the people of God. God gave the spiritual and moral law to the Jews at Mount Sinai, to strengthen their faith in the Lord through obedience to His standards.

In other words, God wants each Jew to acknowledge that He is God. He wants them to humble themselves and repent of their unbelief by putting faith in His promises because He keeps His promises. Then each Jew will want to please God by living by the instructions He has given them, which is called the law.

This creates a personal relationship with God because they love Him and have faith in His promises. This is the kind of relationship Abraham and Moses had with God. Abraham and Moses worshiped and prayed to God alone. They lived to please God. Their obedience to the covenant allowed their love for God to grow into a stronger personal relationship with Him.

Later God gave Moses the Ten Commandments on two tablets of stone (Exodus 31:18). Moses broke them when he saw the golden calf that had been set up in the midst of the camp during his absence (Exodus 32:19). Moses had been on the mount with God for forty days. While he was away, many had turned to the golden calf to worship it. One wonders how they could so quickly have forgotten how God delivered them from Egyptian slavery. Moses had to make two new tablets.

> Then the LORD said to Moses, "Write these words, for according to the tenor of these words I have made a covenant with you and with Israel." So he was there with the LORD forty days and forty nights; he neither ate bread nor drank water. And He wrote on the tablets

the words of the covenant, the Ten Commandments.
(Exodus 34:27–28)

Moses was obedient to serve the Lord and teach the
Israelites the words of God, the Ten Commandments and the
Mosaic laws.

"Obey My voice, and I will be your God, and you
shall be My people. And walk in all the ways that I
have commanded you, that it may be well with you."
(Jeremiah 7:23)

These were God's words to the Israelites who came out of
Egypt, and later God gave the same words to Israel through the
prophet Jeremiah of his day. They are still true today.

"Has the LORD as great delight in burnt offerings
and sacrifices, as in obeying the voice of the LORD?
Behold, to obey is better than sacrifice, and to heed
than the fat of rams." (1 Samuel 15:22)

*God has never cancelled or removed His covenant with
Israel* which includes the Ten Commandments and the law.
Therefore, God's offer, or test, is still open for each Jew today
to have a personal relationship with the God of their fathers.

God's Call to the Judges

The book of Judges is a sad book to read. The Israelites had
to have a leader or they would turn from their covenant with
God and serve idols. Each generation had to learn that serving
Almighty God through His covenant would bring His blessing
and protection.

God always had some Jewish people who had a personal
relationship with Him, but the majority did not understand the
history of their people. They seemed to repeat the rebellion
of previous generations and fail to find their way to receiving
God's blessings by faith.

We will look at two of the judges in this study. The first one
is Gideon.

Gideon

Deliverance had come through the prophetess Deborah and Barak in the battle against King Jabin of Canaan in chapter 4.

So the land had rest for forty years. (Judges 5:31) Then the children of Israel did evil in the sight of the LORD. So the LORD delivered them into the hand of Midian for seven years. (Judges 6:1)

Gideon was hiding in a winepress to thresh wheat so the Midianites would not see him. The angel of the Lord called to him. "The LORD is with you, you mighty man of valor! Gideon said to Him, 'O My lord, if the LORD is with us, why then has all this happened to us? And where are all the miracles which our fathers told us about, saying, 'Did not the LORD bring us up from Egypt?' But now the LORD has forsaken us and delivered us into the hands of the Midianites' (Judges 6:12–13).

Gideon did not understand why God had sold them into the hand of Midianites, so that night God told Gideon, "Take your father's young bull, the second bull of seven years old, and tear down the altar of Baal that your father has, and cut down the wooden image that is beside it; and build an altar to the LORD your God on top of this rock in the proper arrangement, and take the second bull and offer a burnt sacrifice with the wood of the image which you shall cut down" (Judges 6:25–27).

Gideon did what God commanded but he did it at night because he feared the men of the city. The next morning the men of the city learned that Gideon had torn down the image of Baal. They went to his father, Joash, and demanded he hand over Gideon for execution.

But Joash told the men of the city to let Baal defend himself if he was god. Gideon had learned why the Lord had sold Israel to the people of the east. The people of Israel were serving idols instead of God. They wanted to kill Gideon in defense of their idol god.

When Gideon understood the reason God had sold them into the hands of the Midianites, he surrendered to the will of God and acted. Gideon received his answer by experience rather than being told by the angel.

In verse 34, we find that "the Spirit of the LORD came upon Gideon" and he blew a trumpet. He sent messengers out, and called fighting men to come to him.

Gideon sought a sign from the Lord to confirm that the Lord would be with him in the coming battle. He asked that a fleece of wool he placed on the threshing floor would be wet with dew in the morning while the ground around it remained dry. He found the fleece wet and the ground dry, just as he asked. He repeated the request but this time asked that the ground be wet with dew and the fleece be dry. The next morning it was as he had requested.

Thirty-two thousand men responded to Gideon's call. But when they gathered, the Lord let Gideon know he had too many people (Judges 7:2). Those who were afraid were allowed to go home, leaving ten thousand. Then the Lord told Gideon to take the men to the river to drink. He would keep only those who lapped from the water like a dog. Gideon ended up with three hundred men, the number the Lord God wanted (Judges 7:7).

The Lord knew Gideon still had some fear. He said to Gideon: "Arise, go down against the camp, for I have delivered it into your hand. But if you are afraid to go down, go down to the camp with Purah your servant, and you shall hear what they say; and afterward your hands shall be strengthened to go down against the camp" (Judges 7:9–11).

When Gideon and Purah went to the camp of the Midianites, they heard a man describing his dream to his companion. He had dreamed that a loaf of barley bread had rolled into the camp, struck a tent, and the tent collapsed. The second man said, "This is nothing else but the sword of Gideon, the son of Joash, a man of Israel! Into his hand God has delivered Midian and the whole camp" (Judges 7:13–14).

That night Gideon divided his army into three groups so it would appear that the Midianites were surrounded. When Gideon's men blew their trumpets, "the LORD set every man's sword against his companion throughout the whole camp; and the army fled" (v. 22).

God gave a great victory to Gideon and his men. All the credit had to be given to God (Judges 6–7). Gideon judged Israel for forty years.

Gideon is a good example for us today. We may be so busy with life that we do not know the spiritual condition of the nation in which we live. It was clear that Gideon had faith in God but did not understand why his nation was under the control of another nation. By obeying God's instructions, he came to realize how far his people were from trusting in God. Once his belief rested in God, his faith grew and he was obedient to the Lord's will.

As Jews, God may not be sending us to fight a battle, but in His wisdom and care, God is wanting us to humble ourselves and put our faith in Him as Lord. If we do this with all our heart we will be obedient to His instructions.

Samuel

The second judge in this study is Samuel. Before he was born, his mother Hannah had no children so she made a vow before the Lord in the tabernacle in Shiloh. Her vow was that if God would give her a son, she would give that son to the Lord for all his life. She poured out her heart before the Lord. The priest, Eli, heard her prayer and said, "Go in peace, and the God of Israel grant your petition which you have asked of Him" (1 Samuel 1:17).

Hannah had faith in her God and was strengthened by the words of Eli, the priest. The Lord honored her faith and she had a son whom she named Samuel. When he was weaned, she brought Samuel to serve the Lord in the tabernacle. She trained Samuel in the ways of the Lord which made him a blessing to Eli.

Samuel was a boy when he came to live with Eli the priest. As a boy, Samuel wore the linen robes his mother made for him each year. He also wore a linen ephod to minister before the Lord. "And the child Samuel grew in stature, and in favor both with the LORD and man" (1 Samuel 2:26).

All the time Samuel served Eli and the Lord as a child, he was doing what was expected of him by his mother and Eli. At the age of accountability, Samuel had to choose whether or not to serve the Lord of his own free will. "Now Samuel did not yet know the LORD, nor was the word of the LORD yet revealed to him." (1 Samuel 3:7).

One night, God called to Samuel. The first three times He called, Samuel ran to Eli, thinking Eli had called. Eli told him to lie back down. Then Eli realized the Lord was calling Samuel. He told Samuel to respond to the call by saying, "Speak, LORD, for your servant hears" (1 Samuel 3:9). Samuel did as he was instructed. By Samuel's actions one can see he was fully committed to the Lord.

The Lord told Samuel what was going to happen to Eli and his family. The next morning Eli asked Samuel what the Lord had told him. Samuel was faithful to tell Eli all that the Lord told him.

> So Samuel grew, and the LORD was with him and let none of his words fall to the ground. And all Israel from Dan to Beersheba knew that Samuel had been established as a prophet of the LORD.
> (1 Samuel 3:19–20)

The words of Samuel were from the Lord, and what was in his heart from studying God's word were fulfilled by the Lord. Samuel is the first one to be called a prophet by the word of God.

When Samuel came to the age of accountability, he accepted the Lord as his God. Some may think he had no choice because he was in the tabernacle. But Samuel had experienced God's presence and knew the peace that comes to a believer when they trust in God. His commitment was one hundred percent for the Lord.

Samuel serves as an example for us today. The faith of our fathers or mothers is not enough. Each person must humbly accept the Lord as God from the heart. The commitment must be complete. This action will produce faith and be strengthened by studying God's Word and obeying His statues.

Summary of Faith

Like Samuel, one may know the stories of Scripture and believe in the one true God. It is not enough to just believe. There must be a commitment to serve God and trust his Word and covenant. One's faith must be in Almighty God, believing He will do as He has promised.

When Samuel came to the age of accountability, he followed the God of Israel. He was committed to the Lord in all he did and influenced those around him to put their trust in God.

God counted Abraham's faith as righteousness because his actions proved his faith. What a testimony from God himself. "And he believed in the LORD, and He (God) accounted it to him for righteousness" (Genesis 15:6).

Moses tried to help the Hebrews while in Pharaoh's kingdom but had to run and hide. He was eighty years old when God called to him from the burning bush. Moses' commitment had to be a full 100 percent to be effective for God.

Moses had a personal relationship with God which included talking with God one on one. God's presence was in the Israelite's camp throughout their journey. He was in the pillar of cloud by day and the pillar of fire by night. Manna was on the ground every morning except the Sabbath.

The Israelites came out of Egypt by God's strong arm. Their knowledge of God and His presence did not include faith from their hearts to trust and obey His word. Their actions grew out of a self-centered heart of unbelief. Many of the people complained against Moses numerous times and did not recognize God's presence and guidance.

"Therefore understand that the LORD your God is not giving you this good land to possess because of your righteousness, for you are a stiff-necked people. Remember! Do not forget how you provoked the LORD your God to wrath in the wilderness. From the day that you departed from the land of Egypt until you came to this place, you have been rebellious against the LORD." (Deuteronomy 9:6–7)

The people never accepted a personal relationship with the Lord. Their eyes were always on the natural and not on God's presence which surrounded them. As a nation they never put their eyes on the God of Abraham and Moses to serve Him.

The children of Israel were brought out of Egypt by the mighty arm of the Lord. Crossing the Red Sea on dry ground was a miracle that only God could perform for them. When they saw the army of Egypt drowned in the Red Sea and realized God had given Israel a great victory, there was rejoicing in the camp.

God led Israel with a pillar of cloud by day and a pillar of fire by night to the plain before Mount Sinai. God's plan was to give each individual in Israel a covenant to be their God. He spoke from Mount Sinai with His own voice the words of the covenant in the hearing of each Israelite. God's desire was to have a personal relationship with each individual. But they were fearful and rejected God's offer by asking Moses to represent them before God

A personal relationship with God starts when a Jew humbles himself, or herself, believes in God's promises, and accepts the covenant God gave Israel from the Sinai mountain that we reviewed earlier. God said He would show "mercy . . . to those who love Me and keep My commandments" (Exodus 20:6). This is not a one-time commitment to love the Lord but a lifetime of studying God's word and obeying His commandments.

Moses made it clear in Deuteronomy 6:4–5: "Hear, O Israel: The LORD our God, the LORD is one! You shall love the LORD your God with all your heart, with all your soul, and with all your strength."

Let God be the Master of your life and He will direct your path. "He will *love* you and *bless* you and multiply you; He will also bless the fruit of your womb and the fruit of your land, your grain and your new wine and your oil, the increase of your cattle and the offspring of your flock, in the land of which He swore to your fathers to give you" (Deuteronomy 7:13, emphasis added by author).

God desires to love and bless you. But it is conditional on the fact that we love Him, reverence Him, and walk in all His ways. Note the phrase, "in the land of which He swore to your fathers to give you." The nation of Israel has been established since 1948. God is calling each Jew back to the land promised to Abraham's descendants.

> "And now, Israel, what does the LORD your God require of you, but to fear the LORD your God, to walk in all His ways and to love Him, to serve the LORD your God with all your heart and with all your soul." (Deuteronomy 10:12)

Love for God does not stop there.

> "You shall not take vengeance, nor bear any grudge against the children of your people, but you shall love your neighbor as yourself: I am the LORD." (Leviticus 19:18)

Our relationship with God is strengthened as we love our neighbor. This can be a challenge but our Lord will help us.

As a Jew who is the descendant of Abraham, have you put your faith in the promises of God and accepted Him? Also, have you accepted God's call through the covenant He gave to all Jews from Mount Sinai to love Him and make Him your personal God?

The Lord God has never withdrawn His covenant from the children of Israel. Heed God's call and obey His commandments today like Samuel did in his day.

2

The Kingdom of Israel

The last judge of Israel was Samuel but the people wanted a king to lead them so they would be like the nations around them. This displeased Samuel so he went to the Lord in prayer.

And the LORD said to Samuel, "Heed the voice of the people in all that they say to you, for they have not rejected you, but they have rejected Me, that I should not reign over them." (1 Samuel 8:7)

The first man Samuel anointed to be king of Israel was Saul of the tribe of Benjamin. He was the son of Kish, the son of Abiel, the son of Zeror, the son of Bechorath, the son of Aphiah, a mighty man of power (1 Samuel 9:1). Saul was humble at first but pride took its place.

Later, the Philistines gathered their army in Michmash; Saul and his army were camped at Gilgal. Samuel was to come and sacrifice a burnt offering to the Lord. Saul, in his pride, broke God's commandment by offering the burnt offering himself.

When Samuel arrived and found what King Saul had done, he said, "You have done foolishly. You have not kept the commandment of the LORD your God, which He commanded you. For now the LORD would have established your kingdom over Israel forever. But now your kingdom shall not continue. The LORD has sought for Himself a man after His own heart, and the LORD has commanded him to be commander over His people, because you have not kept what the LORD commanded you" (1 Samuel 13:13–14).

The Lord tested King Saul again in chapter 15 of 1 Samuel. Samuel gave King Saul clear instructions to attack the people of Amalek and destroy everything they had because of what the Amalekites had done to Israel. King Saul did attack Amalek, but saved the king as well as the best sheep, oxen, and everything that was good. Samuel, on discovering what King Saul had done by not obeying the Lord, asked Saul why?

King Saul blamed the people for disobeying God's command; he did not repent. Then Samuel informed him that God had rejected him as king over Israel. The Spirit of the Lord departed from King Saul and an evil spirit troubled him (1 Samuel 16:14).

Samuel anointed the second king of Israel at God's direction. The youngest son of Jesse was David who watched the family sheep. "And the LORD said. 'Arise, anoint him; for this is the one!' Then Samuel took the horn of oil and anointed him in the midst of his brothers; and the Spirit of the LORD came upon David from that day forward" (1 Samuel 16:12–13).

The confrontation with the Philistine giant Goliath is recorded in chapter 17. Neither King Saul or any man in Israel would take on the challenge to fight Goliath. The Philistines had set the stage: if Goliath killed the Hebrew who came out against Goliath, Israel would become their slaves. If the Hebrew killed Goliath, the Philistines would become slaves of Israel. The Philistines thought they had the Hebrews cornered because there was no way to defeat their giant.

> Moreover David said, "The LORD, who delivered me from the paw of the lion and from the paw of the bear, He will deliver me from the hand of this philistine." And Saul said to David, "Go, and the LORD be with you!" (1 Samuel 17:37)

Young David, with his sling, selected five smooth stones from a brook as he went out to face the giant. Some believe Goliath had four brothers so David was ready if they came after him. David slung a stone and hit the giant in the forehead. Goliath fell facedown to the ground. Then David

pulled Goliath's own sword and cut off the giant's head
(1 Samuel 17:40–51).

The Philistines did not know there was a young man among
the Hebrews whom God would use because he trusted in God.
Their foolproof plan turned to ashes because of a man led by
the Lord.

Over time, Saul became jealous and afraid of David's
success in battles and of the people's growing admiration for
David. "And Saul was still more afraid of David. So Saul
became David's enemy continually" (1 Samuel 18:29).

In 1 Samuel 19 through 27, King Saul tried to kill David
because of his jealousy of David and to keep his kingdom for
Jonathan, his son. However, King Saul, Jonathan, and two other
of Saul's sons were killed in battle (1 Samuel 31).

David became king in Hebron for seven years, then reigned
in Jerusalem as king of all Israel for thirty-three and a half
years for a total of forty years (1 Kings 2:11). Scripture records
that David was a man after God's own heart (1 Samuel 13:14).
One can see through his writings in the Psalms why God said
this about David.

> Blessed is the man . . . [who's] *delight* is in the law of
> the LORD, and in His law he meditates day and night.
> He shall be like a tree planted by the rivers of water,
> that brings forth its fruit in its season, whose leaf also
> shall not wither; and whatever he does shall prosper.
> (Psalm 1:1–3, emphasis added by author)

> The Law of the LORD is *perfect*, converting the soul;
> the testimony of the LORD is sure, making wise the
> simple; the statues of the LORD are right, rejoicing
> the heart; the commandment of the LORD is *pure*,
> enlightening the eyes; the fear of the LORD is clean,
> enduring forever; the judgments of the LORD are true
> and righteous altogether. More to be desired are they
> than gold, yea, than much fine gold; sweeter also than
> honey and the honeycomb. Moreover by them Your

servant is warned, and in keeping them there is *great reward.* (Psalm 19:7–11, emphasis added by author)

I delight to do Your will, O my God, and Your law is within my heart. (Psalm 40:8)

Take not the word of truth utterly out of my mouth, for I have hoped in Your ordinances. So shall I keep Your law continually, forever and ever; (Psalm 119:43–44)

Oh, how I love Your law! It is my meditation all the day. (Psalm 119:97)

Many more verses express the Psalmist's love and adoration for God's law, statutes, and ordinances. One can see why King David was a man after God's heart. King David serves as an example for every Jew today: man, woman, boy, or girl. Is there any wonder God had the prophet Nathan tell King David his throne would be established forever? "Your house and your kingdom shall be established forever before you. Your throne shall be established forever" (2 Samuel 7:16).

This promise will be fulfilled when the Messiah comes to reign on King David's throne forever. This will be reviewed later in this writing.

Solomon, one of King David's sons, followed David as king. King Solomon built the temple his father had prepared to build. The presence of God in the form of a cloud filled the temple. Later, God visited Solomon a second time.

If you walk before Me as your father David walked, in integrity of heart and in uprightness, to do according to all that I have commanded you, and if you keep My statutes and My judgments, then I will establish the throne of your kingdom over Israel forever, as I promised David your father, saying, 'You shall not fail to have a man on the throne of Israel.' But if you or your sons at all turn from following Me, and do not keep My commandments and My statutes which I have set before you, but go and serve other gods and worship them, then I will cut off Israel from the

land which I have given them; and this house which
I have consecrated for My name I will cast out of My
sight. Israel will be a proverb and a byword among all
peoples. (1 Kings 9:4–7)

God's blessing and protection were conditional. The
descendants had to follow the Lord and be obedient to His
commandments. Moses and all the prophets gave this warning
to their generations as is recorded throughout Scripture. From
the time of Abraham to the building of the temple was around
five hundred years. Each generation had to believe God's
promises and obey His commandments.

God established King Solomon's kingdom with peace on all
sides. God gave Solomon wisdom because that is what he asked
for from the beginning of his reign. God also provided wealth.

Rehoboam, King Solomon's son, became king following his
father. The people ask for the yoke on them to be made lighter
than his father had put on them. King Rehoboam listened to
the men of his own generation and not the wise men who had
counseled his father. Therefore, the ten northern tribes rebelled
and asked Jeroboam to be their king (1 Kings 12).

Northern Kingdom—Israel

Jeroboam said in his heart, "Now the kingdom may
return to the house of David: if these people go up to
offer sacrifices in the house of the LORD at Jerusalem,
then the heart of this people will turn back to their
lord, Rehoboam king of Judah, and they will kill me
and go back to Rehoboam king of Judah."
(1 Kings 12:26–27)

King Jeroboam crafted two golden calves, setting one up
in Bethel and the second one in Dan. "He made shrines on the
high places, and made priests from every class of people, who
were not of the sons of Levi" (1 Kings 12:31). This caused the
people to turn from worshipping the Lord of Israel.

The kings who followed King Jeroboam never removed the golden calves he had set up for worship. Of the nineteen kings who followed King Jeroboam, this study will look at King Ahab. Ahab's father was Omri, who had risen up against King Zimri and attacked Tirzah, the city where the king was located. When King Zimri saw that Omri's forces had taken the city, he went into the citadel of the king's house and burned the house down around him.

King Ahab reigned over Israel for twenty-two years in Samaria. He took as his wife Jezebel, the daughter of Ethbaal, king of the Sidonians, who served Baal.

> Then he set up an altar for Baal in the temple of Baal, which he had built in Samaria. And Ahab made a wooden image. Ahab did more to provoke the Lord God of Israel to anger than all the kings of Israel who were before him. (1 Kings 16:32–33)

Ahab had no respect or fear of the God of Israel. Jezebel killed many of the priests of the Lord (1 Kings 18:4, 13). Her influence even reached into the kingdom of Judah; this will be reviewed in the next section.

Prophet Elijah and Others

Elijah was God's prophet at this time in Israel. Elijah told King Ahab there would be no rain. "As the Lord God of Israel lives, before whom I stand, there shall not be dew nor rain these years, except at my word" (1 Kings 17:1). Then the Lord told Elijah to get away because the Lord knew Jezebel would want to kill him.

After three years of no rain, Elijah challenged Ahab to bring the four hundred fifty prophets of Baal and the four hundred prophets of Asherah under Jezebel to meet him on Mount Carmel. Each group would prepare a sacrifice to their god and the god who answered by fire would be recognized as the true God.

Many in Israel were on Mount Carmel that day to witness the outcome of the challenge. The prophets of Baal and Asherah went first. They spent most of the day praying, crying, and cutting themselves, trying to get their god to answer, but nothing happened.

Then about the normal time of the evening offering in the temple of God, Elijah prepared his sacrifice to Almighty God, the Lord of Israel. He even had water poured three times over the sacrifice. When Elijah prayed, fire came down from heaven and consumed the sacrifice, the wood and stones, and the water around it (1 Kings 18:38).

Elijah ordered that the prophets of Baal and Asherah be killed and it was done. All the people present witnessed the power of God and testified to those who were not present. What a confirmation for all in the kingdom to know God was still wanting the people to return to Him, the only true God.

Jezebel tried to kill Elijah but he escaped and went on doing God's work. Elijah called Elisha to be the prophet of God to follow him (1 Kings 19:19).

Elijah met King Ahab in the garden of Naboth (whom Ahab had killed and whose land he had taken). Elijah delivered God's word to the king.

> I have found you, because you have sold yourself to do evil in the sight of the LORD: "Behold, I will bring calamity on you. I will take away your posterity, and will cut off from Ahab every male in Israel, both bond and free. I will make your house like the house of Jeroboam[3] the son of Nebat, and like the house of Baasha[4] the son of Ahijah, because of the provocation with which you have provoked Me to anger, and made Israel sin." And concerning Jezebel the LORD also

---

3 King Baasha of the northern kingdom "killed all the house of Jeroboam" (1 Kings 15:29).

4 King Zimri of the northern kingdom "killed all the household of Baasha" (1 Kings 16:11).

spoke, saying, "The dogs shall eat Jezebel by the wall of Jezreel" (1 Kings 21:20–23).

By the word of God given through Elijah, the families of Jeroboam and Baasha were destroyed because they would not turn back to the Lord. Now God is telling Ahab the same thing will happen to his family because he will not turn back to the Lord. When Jehu was anointed king of Israel, he fulfilled the words of Elijah (2 Kings 9–10).

It is apparent that the leaders of Israel did not read or try to understand what God had given in His covenant with Israel. They appear to have gone to the synagogue to hear it being read or there may have been no synagogues. No wonder they repeated what were abominations in God's sight, like their fathers.

Moses had received God's law on tablets of stone at Mount Sinai. The Ten Commandments were given in Exodus 20.

I am the LORD your God, who brought you out of the land of Egypt, out of the house of bondage. You shall have no other gods before Me. You shall not make for yourself a carved image—any likeness of anything that is in heaven above, or that is in the earth beneath, or that is in the water under the earth; you shall not bow down to them nor serve them. For I, the LORD your God, am a jealous God. (Exodus 20:2–5)

This is the first commandment of the covenant God made with the descendants of Abraham which is called the law. Each individual in Israel who believed in God's promises and loved His law by obeying it would keep the covenant. If they did not obey the first commandment, the remainder would not be obeyed.

Moses gave Israel clear instructions in writing the book of Deuteronomy. These instructions showed the people of Israel what things should and should not be done when God gave them the Promised Land. This included clear instructions about the idols of the nations in the land of Canaan which they would be possessing.

> You shall burn the carved images of their gods with fire; you shall not covet the silver or gold that is on them, nor take it for yourselves, lest you be snared by it; for it is an abomination to the LORD your God. Nor shall you bring an abomination into your house, lest you be doomed to destruction like it. You shall utterly detest it and utterly abhor it, for it is an accursed thing. (Deuteronomy 7:25–26)

"An abomination," "utterly abhor it," and "accursed thing" means God would not tolerate the images or idols. Some believe it was because demons were involved in the worship of the images or idols. The idols must be destroyed with the material they were made of to protect Israel from being ensnared.

Through the prophets one can see God's warning of coming captivity if His people did not turn from idol worship. Hosea 8:5 holds the key: "Your calf (idol) is rejected, O Samaria! My anger is aroused against them. How long until they attain to innocence (purity)?"

Israel's idolatry led them to rebel against God (Hosea 13:2). The idol was a golden calf erected by Jeroboam, the first king of the ten northern tribes of Israel (1 Kings 12:28–29).

Second Kings 17 records the history of King Hoshea, the last king of Israel, and the fall of the kingdom of Israel. It explains why God sent the king of Syria against Israel.

> There they burned incense on all the high places, like the nations whom the LORD carried away before them, and they did wicked things to provoke the LORD to anger. (v. 11)

Some of the wicked things are recorded in verses 16–18: "They left all the commandments of the LORD their God, made for themselves a molded and two calves, made a wooden image and worshiped all the host of heaven and served Baal.

And they caused their sons and daughters to pass through the fire, practiced witchcraft and soothsaying, and sold themselves to do evil in the sight of the LORD, to provoke Him to anger. Therefore the LORD was very angry with Israel, and removed them from His sight; there was none left but the tribe of Judah alone."

The people of Israel had lived in the Promised Land for more than seven hundred years. God was patient and long-suffering with Israel, but they wanted their own way and their arrogant pride kept them selfish. The people of Israel replaced God's law with the worship of man-made idols and objects of heaven. They may have considered the worship of God to be ancient and old-fashioned. The nation of Israel became very wicked—just like the nations around them. Many of their kings led them into idol worship. God, in His wrath, took the kingdom away from Israel when Assyria destroyed it and took many captives. The prophet Hosea records God's wrath: "I gave you a king in My anger, and took him away in My wrath" (13:11).

Note: God's words were given to Moses who wrote them down for all Jews. Scriptures are God's voice.

Then the king of Assyria carried Israel away captive to Assyria, . . . because they did not obey the voice of the LORD their God, but transgressed His covenant and all that Moses the servant of the LORD had commanded; and they would neither hear nor do them. (2 Kings 18:11–12)

The hearts of the Israelites were not set to worship the Lord by faith and live by His Word. God has given His Word, the law, to let individual Jews know what is required for knowing and serving Him.

God wants more than our outward service through gifts or offerings. Our worship must be by faith, and our service from hearts that desire to know Him and show mercy. How can a person know God without studying His Word? How can a person know what God requires without studying His Word?

How can a person show mercy without committing his or her heart to serving the Lord? God wants a personal relationship with each individual Jew.

> For I desire mercy and not sacrifice, and the knowledge of God more than burnt offerings. (Hosea 6:6)

Now God accused Israel, the northern kingdom, of doing the same things the nations before them had done. God sent Israel, over seven hundred years before, to destroy those nations in the Promised Land because of their wickedness and ungodliness.

Now the ten tribes had become ungodly just like the nations before them. Moses and Joshua and many other prophets had warned them to serve the Lord God of Israel. Otherwise, His anger would make a path for His anger[5], and He would remove them from the Promised Land. It is clear they did not even know God's law because they would have known of the warning.

God warned Israel numerous times through His prophets what would cause His wrath to be aroused against them. The main reasons for God's wrath were the taking advantage of widows and fatherless children (Exodus 22:22–24) and worshipping other gods (Deuteronomy 11:28; Joshua 23:16).

> When the LORD your God cuts off from before you the nations which you go to dispossess, and you displace them and dwell in their land, take heed to yourself that you are not ensnared to follow them, after they are destroyed from before you, and that you do not inquire after their gods, saying, 'How did these nations serve their gods? I also will do likewise.' You shall not worship the Lord your God in that way; for every abomination to the Lord which He hates they have done to their gods; for they burn even their sons and daughters in the fire to their gods. (Deuteronomy 12:29–31)

---

5 This principle was seen in Psalm 78:49–50 when God made a path for His anger, but He prefers or desires mercy (Hosea 6:6).

God tells us in Ezekiel 4:5 that Israel's iniquity was for 390 years. The prophet Ezekiel was in Babylon, taken into captivity in a previous invasion, which proves that God was long-suffering with Israel to get them to repent and return to Him.

> Shalmaneser king of Assyria came up against Samaria and besieged it. And at the end of three years, they took it. In the sixth years of Hezekiah, that is, the ninth year of Hoshea king of Israel, Samaria was taken. (2 Kings 18:9–10)

Israel, the northern kingdom, was destroyed because they had followed the evil ways of the nations around them. sacrificing their children to idols seemed to be the final sin that moved God to pour out His wrath on Israel. Many were killed but some were taken into captivity. Their rebellion had led them into ungodliness, so God removed them from the Promised Land.

The leaders of the northern kingdom serve as examples for those who do not continue to study and obey the voice of the Lord. All Jews must humble themselves and accept the Lord as God and strengthen their faith by studying the Word of God. Then God will help them to live in obedience to His commandments and statutes.

3

The Kingdom of Judah

This section will start with King Solomon, son of
King David, and the third king to rule over all Israel. Solomon
prayed for wisdom[6] but did not ask for riches, long life,
or the lives of his enemies. God gave him wisdom as long
as he walked in God's way by keeping God's statutes and
commandments (1 Kings 3:6–14). King Solomon built an
administration for government affairs like no other king.
He built the temple and all its furnishings for Israel to
worship God in Jerusalem. The Queen of Sheba came to hear
Solomon's wisdom.

When King Solomon became old, he loved many foreign
women. But the Lord had warned His people not to intermarry
with foreigners because their hearts would be turned after
other gods. "His heart was not loyal to the LORD his God, as
was the heart of his father David" (1 Kings 11:4).

Rehoboam, the son of Solomon, became king of Judah
after his father died. King Rehoboam ruled over the southern
kingdom because the ten tribes of Israel rebelled against him.
The kingdom of Judah included the tribes of Judah, Benjamin,
and the people from the northern tribes who wanted to
continue serving God at the temple in Jerusalem. Rehoboam's
mother was Naamah, of Ammons. This helps explain why
King Rehoboam "forsook the law of the LORD, and all Judah
along with him" (2 Chronicles 12:1).

---

6 1 Kings 3:9: "Give to Your servant an understanding heart to judge Your
people, that I may discern between good and evil."

King Rehoboam was forty-one when he became king and he reigned seventeen years. His son Abijam followed as king of Judah. King Abijam "walked in all the sins of his father; . . . his heart was not loyal to the Lord his God, as was the heart of his father David" (1 Kings 15:3). He reigned for three years as king of Judah.

King Asa's Renewal

Asa, the son of Abijam, became king in Judah. King Asa reigned over Judah forty-one years and his "heart was loyal to the LORD all his days" (1 Kings 15:14).

> Asa did what was good and right in the eyes of the LORD his God, for he removed the altars of the foreign gods and the high places, and broke down the sacred pillars and cut down the wooden images. He commanded Judah to seek the LORD God of their fathers, and to observe the law and the commandment. He also removed the high places and the incense altars from all the cities of Judah, and the kingdom was quiet under him. (2 Chronicles 14:2–5)

King Asa also had the priest go to the cities of Judah and teach the people God's law and commandments. God gave King Asa victory over the massive Ethiopian army. As the king returned, the Spirit of God moved on Azariah to speak to him.

> The LORD is with you while you are with Him. If you seek Him, He will be found by you; but if you forsake Him, He will forsake you. But you, be strong and do not let your hands be weak, for your work shall be rewarded! (2 Chronicles 15:2, 7)

> [King Asa] removed the abominable idols from all the land of Judah and Benjamin and from the cities which he had taken in the mountains of Ephraim; and he restored the altar of the LORD that was before the vestibule of the LORD. (2 Chronicles 15:8)

When this work was completed, King Asa gathered the people (those who wanted to seek the Lord) from Judah, Benjamin, Ephraim, Manasseh, and Simeon to Jerusalem. "Then they entered into a covenant to seek the LORD God of their fathers with all their heart and with all their soul" (2 Chronicles 15:12).

Now, one can see why the Lord God said King Asa's "heart was loyal to the LORD all his days" (1 Kings 15:14). The thrilling message to a believer is that King Asa sent the priests and Levites out to teach the commandments and statutes to the people in the cities. The common people heard the voice of the Lord. They seemed to respond to the message better than the people who were at Mount Sinai. Would to God that He would raise up leaders who would do the same in our day.

There was no war in King Asa's kingdom for thirty-five years (2 Chronicles 15:19). The Lord gave peace during this time while the king was cleansing the land and teaching God's law and commandments. God rewarded King Asa as He promised through the word of Azariah for all his effort to turn the people back to the Lord God of Abraham, Isaac, and Jacob (Israel).

King Jehoshaphat's Error

Jehoshaphat, the son of Asa, became king and followed in the way of his father by serving the Lord. King Jehoshaphat was thirty-five years old when he became king, and he reigned twenty-five years. "His heart took delight in the ways of the LORD, moreover he removed the high places and wooden images from Judah" (2 Chronicles 17:6).

One reads in 2 Chronicles 18:1 that Jehoshaphat allied himself, by marriage, with the wicked King Ahab of Israel; this was his *error*. That alliance was made through the marriage of Jehoshaphat's son Jehoram to Athaliah[7], the daughter or niece

---

7 Jehoram married the daughter of Ahab (2 Chronicles 21:6); Jehoram's son Ahaziah was the son of Athaliah, the granddaughter of Omri (2 Chronicles 22:2). Omri was Ahab's father (1 Kings 16:28).

of Ahab, the king who married Jezebel and built a temple in Samaria to Baal the god of Sidon where Jezebel was from.

When King Jehoram was established as king in Judah, he killed all of his brothers which tells us that he had *evil* intent. He walked in the ways of the kings of Israel who did not serve the Lord God but idols made by men. He was thirty-two when he became king, and he reigned eight years. "Moreover he made high places in the mountains of Judah, and caused the inhabitants of Jerusalem to commit harlotry, and led Judah astray" (2 Chronicles 21:11).

Ahaziah, the son of Jehoram, became king in Judah when he was forty-two years old and reigned one year in Jerusalem. King Ahaziah walked in the ways of Ahab his grandfather who was king of Israel (2 Chronicles 22:3). He did not walk in the ways of his grandfather Jehoshaphat. The main reason he did not serve God was because of his mother, Athaliah, the wife of Jehoram, who was related to King Ahab of the northern kingdom.

The prophet Elijah had given King Ahab of the northern kingdom God's word for him and his descendants. "Behold, I will bring calamity on you. I will take away your posterity, and will cut off from Ahab every male in Israel, both bond and free" (1 King 21:21).

About fourteen years later, Elisha gave oil to one of the sons of the prophets. The man was to anoint Jehu king of Israel and give him God's word. The words for Jehu were:

> You shall strike down the house of Ahab your master, that I may avenge the blood of My servants the prophets, and the blood of all the servants of the Lord, at the hand of Jezebel. For the whole house of Ahab shall perish and I will cut off from Ahab all the males in Israel, both bond and free. The dogs shall eat Jezebel on the plot of ground at Jezreel, and there shall be none to bury her. (2 Kings 9:7–8, 10)

It is clear to see that God knows the affairs of individuals. He will judge individuals who do not follow Him but who instead follow their own evil deeds and wickedness. Sometimes that judgment is carried out on this earth. King Ahab and Jezebel behaved as if they would never have to give an account to God for their deeds. Such behavior is called ungodliness. God's judgment may be followed by His wrath. In this case, Jehu carried out God's wrath by cutting off from the earth the descendants of Ahab.

Therefore, King Ahaziah, king of Judah, was a descendant of Ahab. He had come down to see his cousin King Joram of Israel who had been wounded in the battle with Syria. They met in Jezreel of Israel.

The watchman in the city saw a group of men coming to the city. King Ahaziah of Judah and King Joram got into their chariots and went out to meet them. Jehu shot an arrow and it went through King Joram's heart. King Ahaziah fled on the road to Beth Haggan, but was hit by an arrow. He fled to Megiddo where he died (2 Kings 9).

God kept His word to take away the posterity of the house of King Ahab. Even Ahab's grandson, Ahaziah, king in Judah, was removed as Elijah had prophesied. God always keeps His word. One cannot hide from Him.

Athaliah, being the mother of King Ahaziah, made her move to take control of Judah, the southern kingdom, and became queen. Her mother Jezebel had never had the chance to take control of Israel. But now that Athaliah's son was dead, she killed all the royal males (2 Kings 11:1). But Jehosheba, the sister of King Ahaziah, hid one of his sons named Joash and kept him from being killed by Athaliah. Jehosheba was the wife of the priest Jehoiada so they hid Joash in the temple of the Lord (2 Chronicles 22:11–12). Athaliah never entered the temple of the living God.

God had promised David that he would have an heir on his throne forever. God protected Joash, the son of King David as the Hebrew language would call him. God always keeps His

promises. Athaliah tried to break God's promise, but God used
His servant, Jehosheba, to protect Joash, heir to the throne
of David.

Queen Athaliah grew up watching her mother, or aunt,
in her prominent role as leader of the temple in Samaria for
the worship of Baal. She may have dreamed of following her
mother, or aunt, in that role, but such a move in Judah would
have caused a revolt. She must have used her position to set
up elaborate feasts and ceremonies to promote worship of
her gods.

Joash, son of Ahaziah, was hidden in the temple for six
years. Then the priest planned for all the shifts of priests who
served in the temple to be present at one time. He provided
them with weapons to protect the king's son whom they
planned to crown king over Judah.

The day came and all was ready. There was much rejoicing
in the temple to have a son of King David to reign over Judah.

Queen Athaliah heard the sound of the rejoicing and came
to investigate. When she saw the king crowned and the people
shouting, "Long live the king," she cried, "Treason! Treason!"
The captains of hundreds took her outside the temple and
killed her.

Then Jehoiada the priest made a covenant between himself,
the people, and the king, that they should be the Lord's people
(2 Chronicles 23:16). What a wonderful day for those who
followed the Lord God of Israel.

King Joash was seven years old when he became king
and he reigned for forty years. "Joash did what was right
in the sight of the LORD all the days of Jehoiada the priest"
(2 Chronicles 24:2).

When Jehoiada passed away, King Joash no longer followed
the Lord, although he had repaired the temple while Jehoiada
was alive.

> Now after the death of Jehoiada the leaders of Judah
> came and bowed down to the king. And the king
> listened to them. Therefore they left the house of the
> LORD God of their fathers, and served wooden images
> and idols; and wrath came upon Judah and Jerusalem
> because of their trespass. (2 Chronicles 24:17–18)

The great-grandchildren of King Asa's generation were
more than likely leaders of Israel at the time of Joash. Joash
was raised in the temple and protected from the outside world
because he had to be kept a secret to save his life. His spiritual
mentor was dead, and King Joash had to make decisions on
his own. He did not stay loyal to the Lord. It seems he wanted
the approval of the leaders of Israel instead of God. This
compromise was his downfall.

Each generation must put their faith in the promises of
God and follow His commandments. God does not have
grandchildren. This means an individual cannot inherit their
parent's faith but must personally believe in God's promises
and obey His commandments.

The three kings who followed Joash were Amaziah, Azariah
(Uzziah), and Jotham. They did what was right in the sight of
the Lord (2 Chronicles 25:1–2; 2 Kings 15:1–3, 32–34).

The next king was Ahaz. King Ahaz was twenty years old
when he became king and he reigned sixteen years.

> He did not do what was right in the sight of the LORD
> his God, as his father David had done. (2 Kings 16:2)

> He burned incense in the Valley of the Son of Hinnom,
> and burned his children in the fire, according to the
> abominations of the nations whom the LORD had cast
> out before the children of Israel. (2 Chronicles 28:3)

God had sent the children of Israel into Canaan to
destroy and drive out the nations living there because of this
abomination (Deuteronomy 12:31). We saw how God had
removed Israel, the northern tribes, because of this same
abomination.

King Ahaz was the first king of Judah to sacrifice his own son on an altar to an idol. He had seen an altar in Damascus and had one made like it. It was set up in place of the altar designed after the instructions God had given Moses. Maybe Ahaz felt the altar in the temple area was old fashioned and outdated so he had a new altar made. The fact that the old altar was of God's design was of no importance to him.

Committing oneself to God may seem old fashioned to some in a modern world, but God's covenant is the same today and forever until the Messiah comes and sets up His kingdom.

King Hezekiah's Renewal

The son of Ahaz was King Hezekiah. He was twenty-five and reigned twenty-nine years. His mother was Abi (Abijah) the daughter of Zechariah. She was from Jerusalem. "He did what was right in the sight of the LORD, according to all that his father David had done" (2 Kings 18:1–3).

King Hezekiah repaired the house of the LORD and reestablished the priest and Levites for worship in the temple (2 Chronicles 29:3–4).

> He removed the high places and broke the sacred pillars, cut down the wooden image and broke in pieces the bronze serpent that Moses had made; for until those days the children of Israel burned incense to it, and called it Nehushtan.
>
> He trusted in the LORD God of Israel, so that after him was none like him among all the kings of Judah, nor who were before him.
>
> For he held fast to the LORD, he did not depart from following him, but kept the commandments, which the LORD had commanded Moses. (2 Kings 18:4–6)

The Holy Scriptures say King Hezekiah was like his father David. The verses above tell us why: he trusted in the Lord, held fast to the Lord, and never departed from God's commandments and covenant. This is what God wanted from every Jew in each generation. That includes Jews today. What a wonderful testimony for any Jew to have said about him or her.

God knew King Hezekiah's heart and blessed him. The next verses tell us he subdued the Philistines. The Lord prospered him in whatever he did.

It was wonderful for King Hezekiah to destroy the evil idols and high places as he turned Israel back to God. He invited all Jews to keep the Passover feast. His message included: "Do not be like your fathers and your brethren, who trespassed against the LORD God of their fathers, so that He gave them up to desolation, as you see" (2 Chronicles 30:7).

Hezekiah led Judah to keep the Passover in large numbers. Some rejected his invitation. "Nevertheless some from Asher, Manasseh, and Zebulun humbled themselves and came to Jerusalem" (2 Chronicles 30:11).

The term "humbled themselves" is fitting when you think how mighty and holy God is and that He wants a personal relationship with each Jew. Being humble before God is His desire for us.

> So there was great joy in Jerusalem, for since the time of Solomon the son of David, king of Israel, there had been nothing like this in Jerusalem.
> (2 Chronicles 30:26)

In the seventh year of King Hezekiah, King Sennacherib subdued Israel and carried many away to Assyria. In the fourteenth year of King Hezekiah the Assyrian king came against the southern kingdom of Judah. The prophet Isaiah delivered God's word to King Hezekiah that God would turn the Assyrian king around (2 Kings 19). The Lord God rewarded King Hezekiah for turning the people back to the Lord.

The next ruler was Hezekiah's son Manasseh.

> Manasseh was twelve years old when he became king, and he reigned fifty-five years in Jerusalem. . . . He did evil in the sight of the LORD, according to the

abominations of the nations whom the LORD had cast out before the children of Israel. (2 Kings 21:1–2)

And the LORD spoke to Manasseh and his people, but they would not listen. Therefore, the LORD brought upon them the captains of the army of the king of Assyria, who took Manasseh with hooks, bound him with bronze fetters, and carried him to Babylon. Now when he was in affliction, he implored the LORD his God, and humbled himself greatly before the God of his fathers, and prayed to Him; and He received his entreaty, heard his supplication, and brought him back to Jerusalem into his kingdom. Then Manasseh knew that the LORD was God. (2 Chronicles 33:10–13)

Manasseh must have realized when he was taken to Babylon in chains that he was not living right. He humbled himself before the Lord in prayer. God hears the humbled heart that cries out to him; God proved it for Manasseh. Manasseh was brought back to Jerusalem and reestablished as king of Judah.

It is never too late for any Jew to call on the name of the Lord. No matter where you are in relationship with the God of Israel, you can humble yourself by repenting, putting your faith in His promises, and start studying and obeying His commandments; Manasseh proved it.

Manasseh's son Amon was twenty-two years old when he became king of Judah. He reigned two years. "He did evil in the sight of the LORD, as his father Manasseh had done" (2 Kings 21:20). His servants killed him in his own house.

King Josiah's Renewal

King Josiah was eight years old and reigned for thirty-one years. "He did what was right in the sight of the LORD, and walked in all the ways of his Father David; he did not turn aside to the right hand or to the left" (2 Kings 22:2). He was the last king of Judah to follow the Lord with all his heart.

Josiah ordered that the temple be cleansed under the supervision of the high priest (2 Chronicles 34:8–13). During the rebuilding, the high priest found the Book of the Law (2 Kings 22:8).

King Josiah tore his clothes when he heard the reading of the Book. He knew firsthand that Israel was far away from the law of God. The judgments of God prophesied against Judah brought fear upon King Josiah. "Now before him there was no king like him, who turned to the LORD with all his heart, with all his soul, and with all his might, according to all the Law of Moses; nor after him did any arise like him" (2 Kings 23:25).

The cleansing ordered by King Josiah is described in 2 Kings chapter 23. He removed from the temple all the things used to worship Baal and the wooden images. He removed the idols to Baal, the sun, the moon, the constellations, the host of heaven, and their priests from Judah. He made useless the altar where sons and daughters were sacrificed to Molech. He removed the horses used for sun worship and burned their chariots. He defiled the high places Solomon had built to worship the gods of the Sidonians and Moabites and to Milcom. He destroyed the altar Jeroboam built in Bethel. He took away all the high places in the cities of Samaria and killed the priests there.

King Josiah gathered the people from Jerusalem and had the priest and Levites read the Book of the Covenant to the people. This action caused the people to keep the covenant. "All his days they did not depart from following the LORD God of their father" (2 Chronicles 34:33).

Second Chronicles 35 tells of the Passover directed by King Josiah. He and the Jewish leaders provided animals for families to sacrifice in keeping the Passover and the Feast of Unleavened Bread for seven days. The last time Israel had kept the Passover like this was when Samuel was judge (2 Chronicles 35:18).

King Jehoahaz was twenty-three years old when he became king, and he reigned three months. He did not remember the blessings God had given his father Josiah. "He did evil in the sight of the LORD, according to all that his fathers had done" (2 Kings 23:32).

The king of Egypt took Jehoahaz to Egypt and set Jehoahaz's brother Jehoiakim up as king. Judah was forced to pay tribute of one hundred talents of silver and a talent of gold each year. Jehoiakim was made king by Pharaoh Necho at the age of twenty-five, and he reigned eleven years. "He did evil in the sight of the LORD, according to all that his fathers had done" (2 Kings 23:37).

Jehoiakim served King Nebuchadnezzar for three years and then rebelled. Nebuchadnezzar took King Jehoiakim to Babylon along with the articles from the temple of the Lord.

King Jehoiachin was eighteen years old and he reigned three months. "He did evil in the sight of the LORD, according to all that his father had done" (2 Kings 24:9).

When Nebuchadnezzar came against Jerusalem and King Jehoiachin, his family and officers surrendered to the king of Babylon. Nebuchadnezzar carried ten thousand captives to Babylon, including Jehoiachin and his family. It is believed that the prophet Ezekiel was taken to Babylon in the captivity.

The Babylonian king made Jehoiachin's uncle, Mattaniah, king and changed his name to Zedekiah. King Zedekiah was twenty-one years old and reigned eleven years. "He also did evil in the sight of the LORD" (2 Kings 24:19).

In the ninth year of Zedekiah's reign, he rebelled against the king of Babylon. The rebellion was so great that the leaders, including the king, would not listen to the warnings of the prophecies of Daniel, Jeremiah, and Ezekiel. In the eleventh year, Nebuchadnezzar broke through the walls of Jerusalem and destroyed the city. Then they killed the sons of Zedekiah before his eyes, put out the eyes of Zedekiah, bound him with bronze fetters, and took him to Babylon (2 Kings 25:7).

The God of Israel is the same today. If, as Jews, we do not humble ourselves and repent by putting our trust in the promises of God and obeying His covenant, we will suffer loss.

Even though God had evicted Israel from their land in the north because of their iniquity and ungodly worship, Judah did not take heed. About 140 years later—in spite of many prophets calling for them to return and worship God only—God's wrath evicted Judah from their land.

God is calling Jews to believe like Abraham and obey like Moses. Also, He is calling you to your homeland. God is calling all Jews to come home from the second disbursement. You are encouraged to read the rest of this message.

God's Call to Jews Through the Prophets

For this study, the messages calling the Jews were three-fold. The first message was God's call to serve Him and they would receive His blessings and protection. If they continued in their evil ways, God would remove them from their Promised Land.

Second, if the Jews did not turn from their evil ways and come back to the Lord and serve Him, they would suffer loss. Some would be taken captive.

Third, God loved their fathers who served Him and wanted to love them, as well, but they had to repent and obey His commandments. "You shall be holy, for I the Lord your God am holy. . . . Do not turn to idols, nor make for yourselves molded gods: I am the LORD your God" (Leviticus 19:2, 4). This fact is still true now and forever. God gave His people the law and commandments so they could be holy before their God.

God led the people of Israel through the wilderness with a cloud by day and a pillar of fire by night. These were a wonderful blessing for a desert or wilderness. He fed them bread from heaven which they called manna; it was found on

the ground every morning except the Sabbath
(Exodus 16:14, 26, 31). These miracles were all around them
each day.

When they came to Kadesh-Barnea, the people refused to
enter the Promised Land. They rebelled against the direct order
from God. Moses interceded for them (Numbers 14).

May we pause right here? The Lord God of Israel is calling
all Jews to come home. This book is written to help each Jew to
heed God's call.

God put a death sentence on every man aged twenty or
above to die in the wilderness because of their rebellion. The
next generation would possess the Promised Land.

Moses gave the people a warning (Deuteronomy 11:27–
28). The people would be blessed if they obeyed God's
commandments, and they would be cursed if they did not obey.
If the people would not hear the Lord's voice, Moses warned
they would perish (Deuteronomy 30:18–19).

Please note, there is no middle ground for any Jew. It has
never changed. Yes, it is still true today.

Joshua warned God's people against turning away from the
Lord and building an altar for themselves beside the Lord's
altar (22:18–19). Such an altar would be where they would
worship something other than the God of Israel.

"If you turn away your foot from the Sabbath,
from doing your pleasure on My holy day, and call
the Sabbath a delight, the holy Day of the LORD
honorable, and shall honor Him, not doing your own
ways, nor finding your own pleasure, nor speaking
your own words, then you shall delight yourself in the
LORD; and I will cause you to ride on the high hills of
the earth, and feed you with the heritage of Jacob your
father. The mouth of the LORD has spoken."
(Isaiah 58:13–14)

When a Jew keeps the Sabbath and delights in keeping it a holy day, he or she honors the Lord. This brings the blessings of God, especially when that person obeys the rest of the law. Jeremiah 2:13 says God saw Judah as having forsaken Him. He tried to get them to return.

> "If you will return, O Israel, says the LORD, Return to Me; and if you will put away your abominations out of My sight, then you shall not be moved. . . . Circumcise yourselves to the LORD, and take away the foreskins of your hearts, you men of Judah and inhabitants of Jerusalem, lest My fury come forth like fire, and burn so that no one can quench it, because of the evil of your doings." (Jeremiah 4:1, 4)

The circumcision God is talking about here is the removing of everything from their hearts and lives that is displeasing to God and living godly lives. Trust and worship had to be for God alone. In verse 8, Jeremiah says, "For this, clothe yourself with sackcloth, lament and wail. For the fierce anger of the LORD has not turned back from us." Jeremiah is pleading with Judah to repent and turn to the Lord.

In Jeremiah 7, God lists the things Judah was doing to cause His wrath to come on them. Verse 9 lists some of them: "steal, murder, commit adultery, swear falsely, burn incense to Baal, and walk after other gods whom you do not know." Verse 31 says they "burn their sons and their daughters in the fire" to detestable idols. God charges them with more sins than what are listed here. In verse 20, God warns Judah what is going to happen if they do not repent:

> Therefore thus says the Lord GOD: "Behold, My anger and My fury will be poured out on this place—on men and on beast, on the trees of the field and on the fruit of the ground. And it will burn and not be quenched." (Jeremiah 7:20)

They had the example of the northern kingdom.

> I beheld, and indeed the fruitful land was a wilderness, and all its cities were broken down at the presence of the LORD, by His fierce anger. (Jeremiah 4:26)

> I (God) Myself will fight against you with an outstretched hand and with a strong arm, even in anger and fury and great wrath. (Jeremiah 21:5)

God repeats His warning in Jeremiah 21:12; 23:19; 25:15; 30:23; 32:31; 36:7; and 42:18.

God showed His love through His blessing and protection when Israel served Him and kept His covenant. He also says it.

> "I have loved you," says the LORD. "Yet you say, 'In what way have You loved us?' Was not Esau Jacob's brother?" Says the LORD. "Yet Jacob I have loved." (Malachi 1:2)

> I am the LORD, I do not change. (Malachi 3:6)

Ezekiel was a prophet living in Babylon with the captives taken in an earlier invasion. God told Ezekiel that Judah's iniquity was for forty years (Ezekiel 4:6). Even though God sent His prophets to speak to them these forty years, Judah did not heed their call to return to the Lord. Judah did not repent. God told Ezekiel why His wrath would be against Jerusalem.

> "Therefore, as I live," says the Lord GOD, "surely, because you have defiled My Sanctuary with all your detestable things and with all your abominations, therefore I will also diminish you; My eye will not spare, nor will I have any pity." (Ezekiel 5:11)

There can be no doubt as to why the kingdom of Judah suffered God's wrath. Those outside Jerusalem would experience God's wrath (Ezekiel 6:12). The Lord describes in Ezekiel 7 what to expect. "Fury" or "wrath" is used four times to explain what is coming (vv. 8, 12, 14, 19).

> "Therefore I will judge you, O house of Israel, every one according to his ways," says the Lord GOD.

"Repent, and turn from all your transgressions, so
that iniquity will not be your ruin. Cast away from
you all the transgressions which you have committed,
and *get yourselves a new heart and a new spirit.* For
why should you die, O house of Israel? For I have no
pleasure in the death of one who dies," says the Lord
GOD. "Therefore turn and live!" (Ezekiel 18:30–32,
emphasis added by author)

God was calling each individual to *repent* by making Him
their only God, study the law-covenant, and obey it. Then God
would give that individual a new heart and a new spirit which
would lead to spiritual life with Almighty God.

The prophet Ezekiel was in captivity in Babylon and wrote
God's words to Judah. "Now the end has come upon you, and
I will send My anger against you; I will judge you according
to your ways, and I will repay you for all your abominations"
(Ezekiel 7:3).

The ending of the kingdom of Judah was revealed to
Ezekiel. God explained His purpose for sending His wrath
on Judah.

Therefore thus says the Lord GOD: "I will cause a
stormy wind to break forth in My fury; and there shall
be a flooding rain in My anger, and great hailstones
in fury to consume it. So I will break down the wall
you have plastered with untempered mortar, and bring
it down to the ground, so that its foundation will be
uncovered; it will fall, and you shall be consumed
in the midst of it. Then you shall know that I am the
LORD." (Ezekiel 13:13–14)

God was going to use His anger, His fury, His wrath to
remove their greatest defense which was their wall. The
foundation would be exposed with no way to rebuild it.

The prophet Ezekiel lists some of the reasons for God's
wrath in his book and warned them: Judah had idols of Egypt,
defiled the Sabbath, despised God's judgments, rebelled

against God, despised His statutes, caused their firstborn
to pass through the fire, provoked God with their offerings,
committed harlotry, and defiled themselves with all their idols
(Ezekiel 20:8, 13, 16, 21, 24, 26, 28, 30–31).

Ezekiel warned Judah that God's anger, wrath, and fury
were waiting for them if they did not *repent* and turn to the
Lord (Ezekiel 20:8, 13, 33–34; 21:17, 31; 22:20–22, 24, 31;
24:8, 13; 36:18).

> The princes of Judah are like those who remove a
> landmark; I will pour out My wrath on them like
> water. (Hosea 5:10)

They were not honest but deceptive in their positions
as leaders. God was going to use natural disasters and the
Babylonian military to fulfill His wrath. He used the prophet
Amos to warn Israel and Judah.

> Thus says the LORD: "For three transgressions
> of Judah, and for four, I will not turn away its
> punishment, because they have despised the law of the
> LORD, and have not kept His commandments. Their
> lies lead them astray, lies which their fathers followed.
> But I will send a fire upon Judah, and it shall devour
> the palaces of Jerusalem." (Amos 2:4–5)

Amos was calling Judah to repent and return to the Lord
their God: "Seek Me and live" (Amos 5:4). "Seek the LORD and
live" (Amos 5:6).

> And the LORD God of their fathers sent warnings
> to them by His messengers, rising up early and
> sending them, because He had compassion on His
> people and on His dwelling place. But they mocked
> the messengers of God, despised His words, and
> scoffed at His prophets, until the wrath of the LORD
> arose against His people, till there was no remedy.
> (2 Chronicles 36:15–16)

One is left with no doubt regarding why Judah was
destroyed. Their rebellion and wickedness were like that of

Israel's kingdom and Noah's day (Genesis 6:5). The only recourse was God's wrath. God kept His word about what would happen if they did not repent and turn back to Him.

God was patient with Judah by giving them over 140 years to repent and return to Him. Their prophets had referred to Israel as an example because they would not repent; therefore, God had removed them. In their arrogance, Judah did not heed the example of the destruction of the northern kingdom of Israel or the prophets' warnings.

It makes one wonder if they had a false sense of security thinking God would never destroy His temple. They may have respected God's temple, but they did not honor Him in their hearts. They needed a personal relationship with God. Their parents' or grandparents' commitment to God was not enough.

Ezekiel was in Babylon, but the Spirit of God took him to Jerusalem in chapter 8 of his book. In chapter 9, Ezekiel saw the distinction between those who served God and those who would not repent:

> And the LORD said to him, "Go through the midst of the city, through the midst of Jerusalem, and put a mark on the foreheads of the men (people) who sigh and cry over all the abominations that are done within it." To the others He said in my hearing, "Go after him though the city and kill; do not let your eye spare, nor have any pity." (Ezekiel 9:4–5)

The angel of God was marking those who sighed and cried over all the evil in Judah. They would not be killed, but would be taken into captivity when the Babylonian army invaded Jerusalem. God kept alive a remnant who did not partake in the idol worship and evil that filled Jerusalem.

God ordered those who were not marked for captivity to be killed because they were worshipping detestable idols. God destroyed the ungodly and had the righteous taken into captivity. In other words, God removed the abomination from His people.

When the remnant returned to Jerusalem after seventy years[8] of captivity, they never were troubled with idols like before. God cleansed the nation of Israel of the people who would not serve Him. So God cleansed the land of Israel when the Jews came back to their homeland.

Today, God is calling all Jews to their homeland. This call is for each Jew to return with a humble heart and serve the Lord God. There are many examples of people who humbly served God, like Abraham, Moses, David, and the prophets. With the nation of Israel being established for over seventy-five years, the coming of the Messiah to reign on this earth in Jerusalem is closer then ever before. No one knows the date but the signs are all around us.

---

8 Jeremiah 25:11–12; 2 Chronicles 36:21: "Until the land had enjoyed her Sabbaths. . . . To fulfill seventy years."

4

Latter Days

After forty years of wandering around the wilderness, the Israelites came to the border of the Promised Land. Moses wrote the book of Deuteronomy to instruct the people of God. If they chose to study His law and obey it, God would bless the nation and protect them.

Moses' Prophecy

In Deuteronomy 4, Moses commanded the Israelites to obey God's law and warned that idolatry will cause God to scatter them out of their Promised Land.

> And there you will serve gods, the works of man's hands, wood and stone, which neither see nor hear nor eat nor smell. But from there you will seek the LORD your God, and you will find Him if you seek Him with all your heart and with all your soul. When you are in distress, and all these things come upon you in the *latter days*, when you turn to the LORD your God and obey His voice (for the LORD your God is a merciful God), He will not forsake you nor destroy you, nor forget the covenant of your fathers which He swore to them. (Deuteronomy 4:28–31, emphasis added by author)

Note the words "latter days" which give us the timing of this historical event. "When you turn to the LORD your God" may refer to the Jews returning to their land. This was the fulfillment of Isaiah 11:11–12 where God promised to bring Israel back the second time (see the next section of this chapter).

Many Jews started coming back during World War II and following. I remember as a boy reading and hearing how some nations tried to stop the Jews from returning to the land God had given them. But God provided many helps for them to make it to their homeland.

When Israel became a nation on May 14, 1948, the event was fulfilling prophecy. The prophecy was given almost 3,500[9] years before.

> "And evil will befall you in the *latter days*, because
> you will do evil in the sight of the Lord, to provoke
> Him to anger through the work of your hands."
> (Deuteronomy 31:29, emphasis added by author)

There was an event in history that seems to fit this prophecy of "latter days." Six million Jews were murdered by Nazi Germany between 1941 and 1945 during what is called the Holocaust. Many people helped Jews to escape Europe, and the Jews traveled to Palestine.

The League of Nations: the Mandate for Palestine, dated July 24, 1922: "Establishment in Palestine of a national home for the Jewish people."[10] This event led to Jews going to the area commissioned in Palestine to be a national homeland for Jews. Twenty years later many Jews started returning to the homeland God had promised Abraham. God had the land ready, and the nation of Israel was formed in one day, as was prophesied. Let us look at other Scriptures related to this timing.

> For the children of Israel shall abide many days
> without king or prince, without sacrifice or sacred
> pillar, without ephod or teraphim. (Hosea 3:4)

---

9 Edward Hull, *The Wall Chart of World History* (Barnes & Noble Books, 1997)

10 The Israel Forever Foundation. "League of Nations: the Mandate for Palestine," https://israelforever.org/state/Mandate_for_Palestine_Jewish_State/.

The nation of Israel was out of their homeland for 1,878[11] years. This fits the many days in the verse above. They have been back in their homeland for seventy-five years as of the writing of this book.

> Afterward the children of Israel shall return and seek the LORD their God and David their king. They shall fear the LORD and His goodness in the *latter days.* (Hosea 3:5, emphasis added by author)

A number of Jews returning to their homeland are seeking God, and that number continues to increase each year. The population of Jews in Israel is over seven million as of the writing of this book.

In Deuteronomy 4, Moses prophesied that the Jews would return in the latter days. Hosea said they would return and seek the Lord God (chapter 3).

The latter days started when the Jews began coming back to their homeland in the 1940s. The forming of the nation of Israel marks the latter days.

Jews Returning the Second Time

Before we look at the book of Daniel in the next chapter, there is a fact that needs to be established: God promised to bring Israel back to their land after AD 70.

> It shall come to pass in that day that the Lord shall set His hand again the *second time* to recover the remnant of His people who are left, from Assyria and Egypt, from Pathros and Cush, from Elam and Shinar, from Hamath and the islands of the sea. He will set up a banner for the nations, and will assemble the outcasts of Israel, and gather together the dispersed of Judah from the four corners of the earth. (Isaiah 11:11–12, emphasis added by author)

---

11 Israel became a nation in 1948 after being scattered in 70 AD. Therefore, 1948 minus 70 is 1,878

The Jews came back from their Babylonian captivity in 536 BC. They were scattered out of their land in AD 70 when the Roman Empire destroyed Jerusalem and the temple. In the above verse, the Lord is letting us know that He will bring a remnant of the Jews back to their land again. This is termed a "second time." They will come from the whole earth.

> Now the LORD says, who formed Me from the womb to be His Servant, to bring Jacob back to Him, so that Israel is gathered to Him (For I shall be glorious in the eyes of the LORD, and My God shall be My strength), indeed He says, "It is too small a thing that You should be My Servant to raise up the tribes of Jacob, and to restore the preserved ones of Israel; I will also give You as a light to the Gentiles, that You should be My salvation to the ends of the earth." (Isaiah 49:5–6)

This promise is repeated in Isaiah 49:12. God promises to bring the Jews from the ends of the earth back to Israel, their own land. Daniel tells us they will rule with the Messiah when He sets up His kingdom on the earth.

> The wilderness and the wasteland shall be glad for them, and the desert shall rejoice and blossom as the rose; it shall blossom abundantly and rejoice, even with joy and singing, the glory of Lebanon shall be given to it, the excellence of Carmel and Sharon. They shall see the glory of the LORD, the excellency of our God. (Isaiah 35:1–2)

This promise has come to be fulfilled since the Jews started returning to their homeland in great numbers in the 1940s.

> Who are these who fly like a cloud, and like doves to their roosts? Surely the coastlands shall wait for Me; and the ships of Tarshish will come first, to bring your sons from afar, their silver and their gold with them, to the name of the LORD your God, and to the Holy One of Israel, because He has glorified you. (Isaiah 60:8–9)

Years ago, people could not understand the words "fly like a cloud," but we now know they have returned on airplanes and are still returning on airplanes. This prophecy is being fulfilled in our generation.

> Thus says the Lord GOD: "Indeed I Myself will search for My sheep and seek them out. As a shepherd seeks out his flock on the day he is among his scattered sheep, so will I seek out My sheep and deliver them from all the places where they were scattered on a cloudy and dark day. And I will bring them out from the peoples and gather them from the countries, and will bring them to their own land; I will feed them on the mountains of Israel, in the valleys and in all the inhabited places of the country." (Ezekiel 34:11–13).

This promise is repeated in Ezekiel 36:10–24 and 37:21. The phrase "cloudy and dark" means troubled times.

God is calling all Jews (sheep) to their own land. Each Jew must answer God's call individually. God has plans to prepare each Jew for the future of the nation of Israel, to fulfill His purposes. Some of His purposes will be reviewed in the last chapter of this book.

> "Who has heard such a thing? Who has seen such things? Shall the earth be made to give birth in one day? Or shall a *nation be born at once*? For as soon as Zion was in labor, she gave birth to her children." (Isaiah 66:8, emphasis added by author)

God kept His promise by bringing Jews to their land after the Second World War. Yes! A nation of Israel was born on one day—May 14, 1948. God has kept His promise. The Jews, who are God's special people, reestablished the nation of Israel in one day.

Israel retook control of the city of Jerusalem on June 7, 1967. This proves that God is working with the nation of Israel to bring them back to serve and worship Him. The prophecies about Israel in the last days are being fulfilled.

God promised to help the Jews reestablish the Hebrew language. "I will restore to the peoples a pure language, that they all may call on the name of the LORD, to serve Him with one accord" (Zephaniah 3:9).

After 1,878 years, Israel did reestablish the Hebrew language which was nothing short of a miracle because it had never been done in the history of the world. This fact makes us know there is an almighty God and He keeps His promises.

> I will take you from among the nation, gather you out of all countries, and bring you into your own land. Then I will sprinkle clean water on you, and you shall be clean; I will cleanse you from all your filthiness and from all your idols. I will give you a *new heart and put a new spirit* within you; I will take the heart of stone out of your flesh and give you a heart of flesh. I will put My spirit within you and cause you to walk in My statutes, and you will keep my judgments and do them. (Ezekiel 36:24–27, emphasis added by author)

The Lord God may use different methods to lead each Jew back to his homeland. His voice is calling from the pages of His holy Word. This book is only putting His words in modern vernacular and explaining some of the reasons for returning to the Promised Land.

A cleansing is promised by the Lord. He will give each one who puts their trust in Him a new heart filled with His Spirit. This will help each one to obey His statutes and law.

These Scriptures make it clear that the creation of the nation of Israel is by the strong arm of God working in their behalf. In a similar manner, He brought them out of Egypt years ago.

God has kept His promises to the children of Abraham. All the promises from Daniel and the other prophets will come true as surely as Israel was born in one day.

Ezekiel 37 is the prophecy of the dry bones. This is
the prophecy that God will raise up or bring Abraham's
descendants back to the land of Israel.

The Jews' returning to their homeland is the fulfillment of
this prophecy. You are encouraged to read it if you do not know
the prophecy.

There is a reason God is establishing Israel again. Israel
must be in place for the prophecies of the latter days to be
fulfilled. Israel is a key to knowing we are heading into
the end-times.

God has brought the Jews back to their own land using
different methods of transportation, including ships and
airplanes, as the prophecies foretold. As of this writing, the
population of Jews in Israel is reported to be around seven
million. He also reestablished their native language. God has
given Israel control of Jerusalem. This is happening in our
day. God is working with Israel to fulfill the future end-time
prophecies.

What could be next on God's calendar of events for
Israel? Could it be what is written in the next two chapters of
Ezekiel—chapters 38 and 39?

Following Ezekiel's prophecies regarding the Jews' return
to their land comes a prophecy in chapters 38 and 39. This
prophecy reaches fulfillment during the "latter years" recorded
in Ezekiel 38:8 and 38:16. This could well take place in the
time between Israel's becoming a nation and the prophecies of
Daniel which will be reviewed in the next chapter.

> After many days you will be visited. In the *latter years*
> you will come into the land of those brought back
> from the sword and gathered from many people on the
> mountains of Israel, which had long been desolate;
> they were brought out of the nations, and now all of
> them dwell safely. (Ezekiel 38:8, emphasis added by
> author)

Note: the prophecy refers to the mountains of Israel which had been desolate. They are now full of life with Jews dwelling in the land as God prophesied. He has brought many Jews back to their homeland from many nations and continues to bring them back. They have come from around the world to the land of promise. God himself is protecting them.

Gog and the Land of Magog

Gog is the leader or prince of the descendants of Noah's grandsons born to Japheth: Gomer, Magog, Meshech, and Tubal. Included in the descendants is Togarmah the son of Gomer from the far north of Israel. Persia (today's Iran), Ethiopia, and Libya will be part of the invading force with Gog.

> Behold, I am against you, O Gog, the prince of Rosh, Meshech, and Tubal. I will turn you around, put hooks into your jaws, and lead you out, with all your army. (Ezekiel 38:3–4)

In a later verse, God tells us why He will put a hook into Gog's jaw. "I will magnify Myself and sanctity Myself, and I will be known in the eyes of many nations. Then they shall know that I am the LORD." (Ezekiel 38:23)

Prince Gog[12] will develop an evil plan to bring troops and many people in like a storm to cover the mountains of Israel. The prophecy lets us know the plans that are made in secret.

> "You will come up against My people Israel like a cloud, to cover the land. It will be in the *latter days* that I will bring you against My land, so that the nations may know Me, when I am hallowed in you. O Gog, before their eyes." (Ezekiel 38:16, emphasis added by author)

One purpose God has for bringing Gog down against Israel is to hallow His name by His victory over Gog's military. The nations of the world will not have the time, or the desire, to help Israel, but God will prove He is still God.

---

12 God calls this prince Gog in scripture but it may not be his actual name. He may come in the spirit of Gog.

The nations from north of Israel—the descendants of Noah's grandson and the son of Japheth—will be led by a man called Gog from the far north[13] against God's people who are the Israelites. They will come in large numbers to attempt to overpower Israel's military. Their strategy is described in the prophecy. Their armies will come into the land of Israel like a cloud and land on the mountains. Today we know they will come in airplanes along with their military equipment. From this high position, they plan to descend on the unwalled cities and the land of Israel. Gog and his armies will not have considered an almighty God who has made a covenant with His people.

The God of Israel will cause the enemy forces to kill each other as He did of old. This will happen while God is sending rain, hail, and strong winds against Gog and his armies. Gog and his troops will fall on the mountains.

> "I will call for a sword against Gog throughout all My mountains," says the Lord GOD. "Every man's sword will be against his brother. And I will bring him to judgment with pestilence and bloodshed; I will rain down on him, on his troops, and on the many peoples who are with him, flooding rain, great hailstones, fire, and brimstone." (Ezekiel 38:21–22)

Ezekiel 39 gives us more details about the battle.

> You (Gog) shall fall upon the mountains of Israel, you and all your troops and the peoples who are with you; I will give you to birds of prey of every sort and to the beasts of the field to be devoured. (Ezekiel 39:4)

This is repeated in Ezekiel 39:17. The Lord of Hosts will battle against Gog and defeat Israel's enemies.

Gog will be buried in Israel, and it will take Israel seven months to clear the dead bodies from their land. They will use the military equipment and supplies as burning material for seven years.

---

13 Ezekiel 38:15. "You will come from your place out of the *far north*. Also, Ezekiel 39:2 "From the *far north*." (emphasis added by author)

"So the house of Israel shall know that I am the LORD their God from that day forward" (Ezekiel 39:22).

Some believe the prophecy of Gog, from the land of Magog, will be fulfilled in a large battle in the Day of the Lord. The Bible is clear that the final battle with the armies of the world will be in the Kidron Valley or the Valley of Jehoshaphat near Jerusalem, not the mountains of Israel. This will be explained in the next chapter

The battle of Gog is described as taking place in the mountains of Israel. Mountains are referenced six times in these two chapters. The burial place of Gog and his troops will be in the "Valley of Hamon Gog" (Ezekiel 29:11). No other valley is mentioned.

By destroying Gog's military, God proves to all Israel that He is their God. No individual can claim they delivered Israel. God alone will receive the honor and glory for delivering Israel from such a large military force.

Some believe God will cleanse Israel during this time as He did in Ezekiel's day. Remember how Ezekiel, living in Babylon, was taken by the Spirit of God and saw individuals being marked for captivity by an angel because they grieved over the wickedness in Jerusalem (Ezekiel 9:4). The rest of the people were worshipping idols and were killed by the Babylonian army.

God may do something similar at the battle of Gog. Those who refuse to believe and obey the covenant from God given at Mount Sinai would be removed from the land of Israel. Those who believe and obey God's covenant will give God the glory for His great victory.

It appears that God sends fire on the military bases in the homeland of the countries who attacked Israel. "I will send fire on Magog (land of Magog) and on those who live in security in the coastlands. Then they shall know that I am the LORD" (Ezekiel 39:6).

Those nations who come against Israel will have their military bases destroyed. They will know there is a God in Israel.

This will leave a great security vacuum in the Middle East and the countries around it who followed Gog. It would seem possible that the European Union would then increase their military strength to counter the power in the far east, for their own protection. There will be a greater incentive for the countries of Europe to unite politically. This is prophesied in Daniel; they will come to be ruled by ten rulers or super rulers. The King of Deceit[14] will come on the scene about this time and fill the third position created by the Maastricht Treaty of the European Union. This is explained in the next chapter.

---

14 *King of Deceit* is the name this book uses for the final Gentile world ruler. It will become clear in the next chapter.

5

Daniel's Prophecies

King Nebuchadnezzar's Dream

The story of the dream begins in Daniel 2. In the second year of King Nebuchadnezzar's reign, he had a dream that troubled his spirit. He asked his wise men to tell him both the dream and the interpretation of the dream.

The king would not tell the wise men what he had dreamed because he wanted to know the interpretation was true when the wise men told him the dream. The wise men replied that no king had ever asked them to tell what he had dreamed because only the gods, who are not in flesh, could know such a thing.

King Nebuchadnezzar ordered Arioch, the captain of the king's guard, to kill all the wise men. Arioch began carrying out the king's decree. Daniel was one of the wise men who was to be killed. When Daniel asked why such a decree had been made, Arioch told him what had happened.

Daniel went before the king and requested time. Then Daniel and his Jewish companions fasted and prayed earnestly to their God of heaven for the answer to give the king. Their very lives were at stake. They would die along with the other wise men if they did not hear from God.

In a night vision, God showed Daniel a vision of King Nebuchadnezzar's dream but told no one. He wasted no time in requesting to see the king to give the answer to the king's request.

Daniel 2:27–45 gives us Daniel's answer to King
Nebuchadnezzar:

> The secret which the king has demanded, the
> wise men, the astrologers, the magicians, and the
> soothsayers cannot declare to the king. But there is
> a God in heaven who reveals secrets, and He has
> made known to King Nebuchadnezzar what will be
> in the latter days. Your dream, and the visions of
> your head upon your bed, were these: As for you, O
> king, thoughts came to your mind while on your bed,
> about what would come to pass after this; and He who
> reveals secrets has made known to you what will be.
> But as for me, this secret has not been revealed to me
> because I have more wisdom than anyone living, but
> for our sakes who make known the interpretation to
> the king, and that you may know the thoughts of your
> heart.
>
> You, O king, were watching; and behold, a great
> image! This great image, whose splendor was
> excellent, stood before you; and its form was
> awesome. This image's head was of fine gold, its chest
> and arms of silver, its belly and thighs of bronze, its
> legs of iron, its feet partly of iron and partly of clay.
> You watched while a stone was cut out without hands,
> which struck the image on its feet of iron and clay,
> and broke them in pieces. Then the iron, the clay, the
> bronze, the silver, and the gold were crushed together,
> and became like chaff from the summer threshing
> floors; the wind carried them away so that no trace of
> them was found. And the stone that struck the image
> became a great mountain and filled the whole earth.
>
> This is the dream. Now we will tell the interpretation
> of it before the king. You, O king, are a king of kings.
> For the God of heaven has given you a kingdom,
> power, strength, and glory; and wherever the children
> of men dwell, or the beasts of the field and the birds
> of the heaven, He has given them into your hand, and

has made you ruler over them all—you are this head of gold. But after you shall arise another kingdom inferior to yours; then another, a third kingdom of bronze, which shall rule over all the earth. And the fourth kingdom shall be as strong as iron, inasmuch as iron breaks in pieces and shatters everything; and like iron that crushes, that kingdom will break in pieces and crush all the others. Whereas you saw the feet and toes, partly of potter's clay and partly of iron, the kingdom shall be divided; yet the strength of the iron shall be in it, just as you saw the iron mixed with ceramic clay. And as the toes of the feet were partly of iron and partly of clay, so the kingdom shall be partly strong and partly fragile. As you saw iron mixed with ceramic clay, they will mingle with the seed of men; but they will not adhere to one another, just as iron does not mix with clay. And in the days of these kings the God of heaven will set up a kingdom which shall never be destroyed; and the kingdom shall not be left to other people; it shall break in pieces and consume all these kingdoms, and it shall stand forever. Inasmuch as you saw that the stone was cut out of the mountain without hands, and that it broke in pieces the iron, the bronze, the clay, the silver, and the gold— the great God has made known to the king what will come to pass after this. The dream is certain, and its interpretation is sure.

After hearing Daniel, King Nebuchadnezzar declared: "Truly your God is the God of gods, the Lord of kings, and a revealer of secrets, since you could reveal this secret" (Daniel 2:47).

The king's attention and attitude must have told Daniel that he had accurately described the dream. When he used the words "certain" and "sure" while giving the interpretation of the dream, he must have felt the anointing of the Spirit of God like the prophets of old. As we read it today, God's Spirit confirms in our hearts that they are God's words.

Gentile World Rulers

It is interesting that the Lord had given the dream to a heathen king and not to one of the kings of Israel. This may have been because Nebuchadnezzar was the first Gentile government to rule the known world at that time. Also, he had a wise man who was totally surrendered to Almighty God by living out the covenant God had made on Mount Sinai. Daniel prayed three times a day because he had a personal relationship with God. He was used in the interpretation of the dream because the Lord knew Daniel would give the entire honor to God.

God allowed King Nebuchadnezzar to see, through the image, the Gentile kingdoms that would rule the world after his reign. Each kingdom was illustrated by a metal substance (except the baked clay), which tells us something about those kingdoms. The metals decreased in value from the head to the foot of the image. The kingdoms were known for their emphasis on and abundance of these metals.

If humans describe a building or structure, they usually start at the foundation and go up. God started at the top and went down to illustrate the kingdoms to the last Gentile kingdom.

Daniel described the kingdoms in terms the people of Babylon would understand. Each kingdom would rule the center of the world for a specific period of time. Each kingdom would not completely destroy the previous kingdom, but would build on its wealth and power. Many of their laws and philosophies were carried on as well.

The Babylonian Empire became dominant in the world under Sennacherib in 705 BC[15]. The Babylonian Empire lasted about 167 years until the Media-Persian invasion in 538 BC.[16]

The year King Nebuchadnezzar had the dream was about 600 BC. Daniel identified King Nebuchadnezzar as the head

---

15 Hull, *The Wall Chart of World History.*

16 Not all historians agree on the dates of history; please do not get hung up on dates.

of gold depicted in the image. Nebuchadnezzar was the most dominant king of the Babylonian Empire.

God shows us that Babylon was the first Gentile kingdom to dominate the world. Under the next section, "Daniel's Visions," we will see in Daniel 7 that King Nebuchadnezzar is depicted as a lion with four eagle wings.

The Medes and Persians, represented by the chest and two arms in the image, invaded Babylon and were victorious. This second kingdom was the Persian Empire which lasted 229 years, from 559 BC to 330 BC. Daniel said the two arms and chest were made of silver. This empire is depicted as a bear in Daniel's vision of chapter 7.

The third kingdom, represented by the belly and thighs of bronze, was the Greek Empire. Alexander the Great became king in 336 BC at the age of twenty. He had conquered the known world by the age of thirty-three. He died in 323 BC. This time was known as the Bronze Age. This empire is depicted as a leopard in Daniel 7.

After the death of Alexander the Great, a civil war broke out as his generals vied for control of the kingdom. By 320 BC, the Greek Empire was divided into two kingdoms, each led by one of the original generals. This division is depicted in the image by the thighs. The two power centers are considered to be the East and the West. That division is still present today. However, in Daniel 11, the two kingdoms are called the North and the South.

During this time, the fourth kingdom was increasing in strength in Rome. By 146 BC, the Greek Empire had become a province of Rome. Daniel described this fourth kingdom as being made of iron and consisting of the legs of the image. The iron kingdom, the Roman Empire, crushed and shattered the kingdoms they conquered (Daniel 2:40). It is described as dreadful and terrible in the vision of chapter 7.

The Roman Empire continued to conquer nations. In 27 BC, Augustus Caesar became the first emperor of the

Roman Empire, a time identified in history as the Golden Age of Rome. The Roman Empire ruled over more territory than any of the other world powers before them. They ruled more years than any of the prior world powers. They ruled with an iron fist from a basis of law and order. The Roman Empire's law was forced on the nations they conquered.

The dominance of the Roman Empire lasted about 422 years. If one was to count from the conquering of Greece to the dividing of the Roman Empire, the total would be about 541 years.

Daniel did not say any other kingdom or empire would take over the fourth kingdom, the Roman Empire. The iron continues down into the feet. In the feet, the iron is mixed with ceramic clay. The feet started in AD 395 when the Roman Empire broke into many nations under Theodosius I who divided the empire. When reading about the Roman Empire, one cannot help but read about the division of the East and West. It still dominates the world today. For more than 1,600 years, the world has consisted of many nations with no world kingdom or empire. This period of time is the feet of the image of Daniel 2.

We are living in the time of the feet today. God does not give us a time limit for this period. The feet will end when the ten toes appear. The ten toes, or the ten kings or rulers, who will build an empire that influences the whole world from Europe is still in the future.

History has recorded in detail the prophecies Daniel described to King Nebuchadnezzar about the image in the dream he received from God. The Gentile nations have dominated the ruling of earth just as Daniel's prophecy foretold. This would indicate that the rest of the dream's interpretations will come true just as accurately as the first ones.

Daniel 2:41 tells us about the feet and toes of the image. They are made of ceramic clay and iron. Each nation or kingdom will be divided, but the strength will be in the iron which is represented by law and order.

The image is standing on the feet so there is strength in the feet. The iron and ceramic clay are divided and distinguishable from each other. They hold the whole image in its place. They have a different consistency from each other. Iron is rigid and hard, and ceramic clay is brittle. The iron would denote a strong center of government based on law and order. This is consistent even when leaders change. The clay would denote a soft center of government where law and order changes with each new leader and has no consistency.

These are the kinds of governments that have existed around the world since AD 395. No empire has conquered the world after this date. There have been those who have tried, such as the Saracens, Hitler, and Communism, but none have been able to repeat what the Roman Empire was able to do—just as Daniel explained in the interpretation of Nebuchadnezzar's dream.

However, Daniel prophesied of two more future world leaders. Their kingdoms are defined within their time frame.

Ten Toes: Future

The last part of the image referred to is the toes. The toes are made of iron and ceramic clay, the same as the feet. Daniel 2:42–43 lets us know the people of the various nations will not mix; just like the clay and iron, they will not be united. The materials do not mix with each other just as the people will not unite. The image has two feet, one under each leg, which shows the same condition in the East and the West. The East and West are still divided. The effects of the Macedonian Empire or Greek Empire are still with us today.

In Daniel 2:44, the toes are referred to as kings. There will come a time when ten kings or rulers will have immense power over the world. Since the Macedonian kingdom and the Roman Empire were both in Europe, we would expect the ten kings or rulers to be from the same area of the world. The distinction between the toes is seen by following the legs and feet and tells us that the kings or rulers will be from the East and West.

The capital of the Roman Empire was in Europe. For now, there will be a government that will have as its central governing power ten kings or super leaders (same number as the toes), and they will have power and influence over the world. This power and influence will not be the same as the Roman Empire, but will be similar in power and scope at the start.

As of this writing, there is a European Union on the continent of Europe. This could be the embryo of the future ten kings or ten rulers that Daniel refers to as the ten toes. If this is the last Gentile government forming, then we are through the feet of the image and close to the toes. This subject will be discussed later in this chapter.

Daniel tells us what happens after the reign of the ten-toe kingdom (Daniel 2:44–45). The God of heaven will set up a kingdom that will never be destroyed, and God's ruler will rule until the end of time. He will destroy all earthly kingdoms and take nothing from them. This Ruler will be the Messiah.

> I will declare the decree: The LORD has said to
> Me, "You are My Son, today I have begotten You.
> Ask of Me, and I will give You the nations for
> Your inheritance, and the ends of the earth for Your
> possession. You shall break them with a rod of iron;
> You shall dash them to pieces like a potter's vessel."
> (Psalm 2:7–9)

The "stone" (Daniel 2:45) that was cut out of the mountain without hands is the Messiah. The Messiah will set up His kingdom on this earth and rule the entire world. The Gentile kingdoms built their cultures and political systems upon the ones they conquered. When the Messiah sets up His kingdom, all the Gentile systems will be done away with. There will be no trace of the Gentile kingdoms. The reason for this is that the Messiah's kingdom will be built on righteousness and holiness.

When one understands that God has everything planned for humanity, there is peace of mind. All Scripture is given so we can understand God's plan for salvation. If we choose Him, our future destination is with Him for eternity. We do not have to question where we will spend eternity if we have repented and turned to the Lord God and His covenant.

God is never surprised with events on this earth. We can see, by this study, that all is planned by our Lord God. Therefore, it is imperative that we study the Word of God.

We can see that the interpretation of the dream that Daniel received from God has come true to this point. Since the Roman Empire's demise, we have seen the iron and clay governments. We have assurance that the rest of the dream will come true, just as Daniel told it.

Daniel gave an overall outline of the Gentile governments. With this overview, it is easier to understand other Scriptures because we can see how they fit into the overview. When you stand on a mountaintop and look down a range of mountains, you do not see the valleys between the mountains. Scripture is the same on many subjects, and those subjects include end-time events. We see the highlights, but not what is between.

From this study so far, we understand we are presently living in the feet of the image. Since God allowed the Jews, His chosen people, to establish their nation as Israel in 1948, we are near to the toes of the image coming into existence. Therefore, the next big event from the image is the development of the ten toes—the ten kings or rulers. Could the coming together of the European nations into the European Union be the beginning or the embryo of the ten toes? This is worth watching.

God laid the framework of this dream for each generation to show He has everything under control. God is in control—not any other person or being—which gives believers the peace that only God can give.

A diagram of Daniel's dream (chapter 2) is provided in Figure 1 on the following page. An actual image is not drawn, but the parts of the image are placed to fit the image of a man. This image will depict the words we have studied. The visions of Daniel in later chapters are included.

Figure 1
Nebuchadnezzar's Dream and Daniel's interpretation
(Daniel 2:1, 19, 27–45)

GENTILE GOVERNMENTS

Head of Gold

Babylon Empire
Head of gold is King Nebuchadnezzar
(Daniel 2:32, 36–38)
Lion with wings
(Daniel 7:4, 17)

Chest and
Two Arms
of Silver

Media-Persia Empire
Chest and arms of silver
(Daniel 2:32, 39)
Bear with 3 ribs
(Daniel 7:5, 17)
Ram with two horns
(Daniel 8:3–7, 20)

Belly and Thighs
of Bronze

Greece Empire
Belly and thighs of bronze
(Daniel 2:32, 39)
Leopard with 4 wings, 4 heads
(Daniel 7:6, 17)
Male goat with 1 horn/4 horns
(Daniel 8:5–8, 21–22)

Legs of Iron

Roman Empire
Legs of iron
(Daniel 2:33, 40; 7:7, 19, 23)
Many nations in world

Stone cut out of mountain
without hands destroys the
image
(Daniel 2:34–35, 44–45)

Feet of Iron/Clay

Feet of iron and ceramic clay
(Daniel 2:33, 41; 7:7)

FUTURE

Stone is
Messiah

Toes of Iron/Clay

Or **10 Horns–Rulers/Kings**
New "European Empire"[17]
Iron mixed with ceramic clay
(Daniel 2:42–43; 7:8, 20)
Little/other horn, a king
(Daniel 7:8, 11, 20–21, 24–25)
(Daniel 8:9–12, 23–25)

Stone becomes a mountain,
fills the whole earth which is
the **kingdom of God**—
righteousness. (Messiah)
(Daniel 2:34, 44–45)

---

17 The title "European Empire" is used because one does not know what they will call
themselves in the future, but it will be in Europe.

In studying Daniel 2, we have looked at more than 2,600 years of history regarding Gentile governments that ruled this world. Daniel's interpretation has come true up to and including the feet of the image. The details were more than sufficient to see the fulfillment of these prophecies. Therefore, it is reassuring to understand the future prophecies will be completed just as those we have reviewed.

Israel's becoming a nation again on May 14, 1948, lets us know God is working to complete the prophecies regarding Israel. Now that God has brought many Jews back into their own nation, we know Gentile kingdoms will come to an end.

The last ruling Gentiles of the world will be in the ten toes of the image described in Daniel 2. When the ten rulers have ruled a short time, the King of Deceit will take over their power and rule the world for seven years. This prophecy will be fulfilled because God has declared it. Following will come the Stone which is the Messiah. He will set up the kingdom of righteousness that will never be destroyed.

Later in Daniel's life, he had visions in which God provided more details about the Gentile kingdoms and their leaders. These visions give us much more information about these governments and their leaders, which we can see fulfilled in history. For those prophecies still in the future, the information God gave through Daniel provides an outline of what to expect. God also gave a timetable for the latter days and end-times of the Gentile kingdoms. We provide this information in Table 2 toward the end of this chapter.

Daniel's Visions

The Lord gave Daniel a vision in chapter 7, about sixty years after the dream in chapter 2. Daniel spent a night in a lion's den in chapter 6, and God delivered him. His faith was severely tested, but God brought him through. His faith had been built on reading and studying the Word of God and praying to God three times a day. He met with other believers to pray. We build our faith the same way by assembling with other believers.

Daniel's first vision is recorded in chapter 7. In this vision, God showed Daniel a sequence of four beasts that came up out of the Great Sea. Many scholars interpret the sea as being the masses of humanity. Therefore, the four beasts were men who came from the masses of humanity as leaders in their time.

The vision is recorded in the first fourteen verses of chapter 7, which we will review first. The interpretation is in the last thirteen verses. It covers the same subjects as the dream in chapter 2, but provides more details about the leaders and their kingdoms.

The first beast was like a lion with four eagle wings. This beast represented King Nebuchadnezzar, the first Gentile king to rule the world. King Nebuchadnezzar was general of the Babylonian army when they conquered the nations around them. In the image of chapter 2, he was the head of gold. He swiftly conquered one nation at a time, which the wings represent, as he ascended to the status of world leader in the Babylonian Empire. In chapter 4, Daniel tells how God humbled King Nebuchadnezzar. In chapter 7, he was made to stand on the earth as a man and was given a man's heart (v. 4).

The second beast was like a bear. It represented the Persian Empire and the Medians. The three ribs between its teeth could easily be the territories the Persian Empire conquered: Asia Minor, the Medes, and the Egyptians. The vision describes this empire as devouring much flesh. This empire corresponds with the chest and two arms of silver of the image. Persia conquered Babylon with the help of the Medians, but they soon became the dominant power of the world at that time (Daniel 7:5).

The third beast was like a leopard with four wings like a bird. It conquered kingdoms quickly. This would be the belly and thighs of bronze of the image and represented the Greek Empire led by Alexander the Great. He had conquered the known world by the age of thirty-three. The leopard had four heads into which Alexander the Great's four main generals divided the Greek Empire upon Alexander's death (Daniel 7:6).

The fourth beast was terrifying, dreadful and very powerful. It had huge iron teeth that devoured, broke into pieces, and trampled the residue under its feet. This represents the legs of iron in the image of chapter 2. The fourth beast represented the Roman Empire (Daniel 7:7).

Daniel writes more about this beast because it was so different from the other beasts. Daniel could find no other animal to liken it to. He spent more time describing its features because they stood out to him. Each feature had a meaning. The interpretation of the details Daniel received lays the groundwork for understanding other prophecies.

This beast which came up last had ten horns which made it different from the other three beasts. As Daniel watched, a little horn came up and uprooted three of the original horns. The little horn had eyes, a mouth like a man and spoke pompous words (Daniel 7:8).

Then the Ancient of Days took His seat, and the books were opened (Daniel 7:9–14). He slew the terrifying beast, and the Messiah was given the kingdom of this earth never to be destroyed. The Stone in chapter 2 which struck the image's feet and toes is the Messiah. The Lord gave the authority, glory, and sovereign power of all nations to His Ruler.

Interpretation of Daniel 7

The interpretation of the dream starts in verse 17. Daniel is told the four beasts are four kings who rule the world. The final kingdom will be given to the believers who put their full trust in God, who created this world. Their kingdom will have no end (Daniel 7:17–18).

Daniel gives more details about the fourth beast with iron teeth, nails of bronze representing its power to conquer. The iron legs enable the beast to trample the residue. The ten horns of this beast come up last or in the end-times. They are represented by the ten toes of iron and ceramic clay of the image. The ten horns and the ten toes of the beast speak of the last Gentile government to rule the world. This lets us know the ten kings or rulers are from the base or this area of the world, which is the fourth beast. We will see that their time of ruling is limited.

"The ten horns are ten kings who shall arise from this kingdom" (Daniel 7:24). The ten kings would come from the fourth beast or the last world power, representing the Roman Empire, which Daniel was shown in chapter 7. This explains where the ten toes or horns come from in chapter 2. By following the iron in the legs down the image into the feet and toes, one can see that the ten toes or ten horns are from the fourth beast. In other words, the ten toes are the same as the ten horns in number and from the same kingdom. They will come out of the feet, from the same area of the last two beasts, located in Europe.

Therefore, the last Gentile Empire will be a revised Roman empire called by a different name. The European Union may be the embryo of this government. If so, it will become clear when we see ten super leaders given full governing power in the European Union or European Empire (term used for this study).

Daniel saw in his vision that a small horn appeared and uprooted three of the original ten horns. This horn (called the King of Deceit in this study) had eyes like a man and spoke pompous or boastful words: "He shall speak pompous words against the Most High" (v. 25).

This last horn is different from the others, and he will make war against the Jews or saints. Verse 25 tells us the time limit on his war against the Jews—"for a time and times and half a time"—which is three and a half years. He will prevail until the Ancient of Days, the Most High, comes with judgment on the small horn and destroys him. Then the Messiah is given the kingdom over all the earth.

The Stone (Messiah) of the dream in chapter 2 is found in the interpretation of chapter 7.

Then the kingdom and dominion, and the greatness
of the kingdoms under the whole heaven, shall be
given to the people, the saints of the Most High. His
kingdom is an everlasting kingdom, and all dominions
shall serve and obey Him. (Daniel 7:27)

The saints of the Most High are the believing Jews who will
reign with the Messiah from Jerusalem.

The second vision is described in chapter 8. Daniel had a
vision of a ram and a male goat. The ram had two horns which
were the Medes and the Persians, but one horn was higher than
the other and after some time became the Persian Empire. The
ram became great. No animals were able to withstand him
(Daniel 8:3-4).

A male goat—the Greek Empire—with a large horn between
his eyes—Alexander the Great—came from the west. He came
so swiftly he did not touch the ground.[18] The male goat attacked
the ram and overpowered him, and no one was able to help the
ram. At the height of the goat's power, its horn was broken off,
and four notable horns replaced it. The four generals were the
horns that tried to take the kingdom but did not have the same
power as the first horn.

Out of one of the horns of the four Greek generals another
little horn came up and grew in power to the south and east
(Daniel 8:9). He exalted himself above everyone including
the "Prince of the host," God. This little horn was filled with
transgressions, and an army was given to him. He stopped the
daily sacrifices and cast down the sanctuary. This little horn was
the King of Deceit. He cast truth down and prospered, but after
2,300 days the temple was cleansed. The Messiah will cleanse
the temple when He comes to reign.

---

18 This is the third beast, described as a leopard with four wings like a bird in
Daniel 7:6, and as a male goat in 8:5.

Interpretation of Daniel 8

Gabriel, a mighty angel of God, gives Daniel the interpretation of the vision in 8:16–17. The interpretation Gabriel gives Daniel includes a prophecy.

> The vision refers to the *time of the end*. . . . And he said, "Look, I am making known to you what shall happen in the *latter time* of the indignation; for at the appointed *time the end* shall be. (Daniel 8:17, 19, emphasis added by author)

The latter time is reviewed in chapter 4 of this book. The "time of the end" refers to when the last Gentile kingdom will rule the world. Therefore, the prophecy of the little horn is referring to the last Gentile leader, who will rule at the end of the last Gentile Empire—the King of Deceit. This makes it very clear that the little horn is from the male goat or the Greek Empire. We will review more about this ruler later.

It is worth noting that the word "indignation"[19] in verse 19 refers to God's wrath in the Day of the Lord at the end of the last Gentile empire. It is still the future for us.

The last Gentile government is referred to in the phrase "in the latter time of their kingdom" (v. 23) which will be the ten toes made of ceramic clay and iron. The little horn represents the King of Deceit who will rise to rule the world through the last Gentile government and replace the ten rulers who will only rule for a short time.

The iron from the last world kingdom is represented by the iron in the legs of the image in Daniel 2. The iron in the legs continues into the toes but is mixed with ceramic clay. Therefore, the last Gentile government will be in Europe but will have a new name like the European Empire. Greece is part of Europe and will be part of the new European Empire (Daniel 8:23).

---

19 *Za'am*: fury wrath. John R. Kohlenberger III and James A. Swanson. *The Strongest Strong's Exhaustive Concordance of the Bible, Large Print Edition.* (Grand Rapids, MI: Zondervan, 2002), Hebrew reference 2195.

Daniel 8:23–26 is referring to the last Gentile ruler of the world. The end of the Gentile kingdoms is marked by the phrase "latter time of their indignation" (God's wrath) poured out at the end of this kingdom. It is not the end of the world; it is the end of the rule of the Gentiles. In the image of Daniel 2, this government is the ten toes (Figure 1).

The ram with two horns represented the kings of Media and Persia. Persia, the horn that was higher, became the dominant power of this cooperation (Daniel 8:20).

The male goat was the Greek Empire. The male goat with one large horn between its eyes is the first king, Alexander the Great. He conquered the kingdom of Persia and all others by the age of thirty-three. History tells us he lamented because he had no other kingdoms to conquer. Daniel says this horn was broken off, which speaks of his death.

The four horns that replaced the one large horn between the eyes were the four prominent generals from the four winds of heaven. The four horns did not have the same power because the kingdom was divided (Daniel 8:21–22). The four horns are the same as the four heads on the leopard in chapter 7.

Out of these four generals, two become dominant in chapter 11 as the king of the North and the king of the South. The end result sets up the division of the East power struggle and the West power struggle. They are represented in the thighs of the image of chapter 2.

In the end-time, or the days of the last Gentile government, a king will rise from the area of the male goat, or Greece, which has become full of transgressors. These transgressors will come from a wicked people. The king or political leader will understand sinister schemes or the art of deception. This leader is the King of Deceit. This second vision is letting us know the King of Deceit, himself, will come from the third beast or from the Greek Empire.

The King of Deceit will have mighty power but not of his own making. He will be empowered by the evil one, and will cause deceit to prosper. He will destroy many, including some Jews, and exalt himself. He will even try to stop God from setting up His kingdom of righteousness (Daniel 8:25).

The phrase "sinister schemes" (v. 23) refers to a time when leaders have no thought of God or fear of answering to Him. It appears we are in the beginning of this time period. Wicked people will support a fierce-looking king who will be a master of secret influences—the ability to masterfully deceive. He will be strong because of the indwelling or influence of the evil one; it will not be human power. We are told he will prosper and be very arrogant.

Therefore, Daniel 8 lets us know that the King of Deceit will come from the base of the third Gentile kingdom, the Greek Empire. He will come to rule the world by taking authority from the ten rulers of the European Empire. Again, God has set a time limit on the reign of the King of Deceit. The limit will become clear later.

Interpretation of Daniel 9: Seventy Weeks

Daniel's prayer is recorded in chapter 9, verses 4–20. His prayer was accompanied with fasting to humble himself before God. He repented of his sins and the sins of his people and petitioned God for mercy, forgiveness, and the restoration of his people back to Jerusalem. Remember, Daniel prayed three times a day. He studied Moses' and the prophet's writings. While he was praying, Gabriel, an archangel, came to him directly from God to deliver God's message to him (vv. 21–23).

> Seventy weeks are determined for your people and for your holy city, to finish the transgression, to make an end of sins, to make reconciliation for iniquity, to bring in everlasting righteousness, to seal up vision and prophecy, and to anoint the Most Holy.
> (Daniel 9:24)

God decreed "seventy weeks" of seven years or "a unit of time in the book of Daniel, possibly a 'week' of seven years"[20] for a total of 490 years (seventy times seven years). This was for the Jewish people only—not the world or any other peoples. Daniel was a Jew, and this prophecy was for the Jews and their holy city Jerusalem.

Two examples help us understand the units of seven years. The first is Jacob's marriages. Jacob labored for a week of seven years to marry Rachel. Laban, Rachel's father, gave him Leah, his oldest daughter instead. Then Jacob labored another week of seven years to marry Rachel (Genesis 29:21–30).

The second example is found in Leviticus 25. Israel was to work the land for six years, but the seventh year was to be a sabbath year of rest for the land (vv. 3–4). They were to count seven sabbaths of years times seven sabbaths of years to a total of forty-nine years, with the fiftieth year to be their year of Jubilee, a year of liberty. Israel was accustomed to a week of seven years (vv. 8–13).

Gabriel gave Daniel two different periods of time within the 490 years of seventy weeks. Let's look at each one separately.

First Time Period: Sixty-Nine Weeks

> Know therefore and understand, that from the going forth of the command to restore and build Jerusalem until Messiah the Prince, there shall be seven weeks and sixty-two weeks; the street shall be built again, and the wall, even in troublesome times. (Daniel 9:25)

Seven weeks of years and sixty-two weeks of years make a total of sixty-nine weeks of years. The sixty-nine weeks of seven years make a total of 483 years (sixty-nine times seven years).

---

20 "Weeks" means a unit of seven years in the book of Daniel. Kohlenberger III and Swanson, *The Strongest Strong's Exhaustive Concordance of the Bible*, Hebrew reference 7620.

The event that starts this period is when King Artaxerxes I of Persia decreed that Nehemiah rebuild the walls and streets of Jerusalem in approximately 450 BC.[21]

When the 483 years were complete, the Jews in Israel had no personal relationship with God. The elders and scribes of Israel had added many ordinances, well over six hundred, to the law or covenant God had given the Jews at Mount Sinai. The nation of Israel had lost their commitment to God's law and instead followed the ordinances.

> And the people of the prince who is to come shall destroy the city and the sanctuary. The end of it shall be with a flood, and till the end of the war desolations are determined. (Daniel 9:26)

The people of Israel were not ready for the Messiah. God sent the Roman army (the prince) to destroy the city and the temple. This happened in AD 70. The people of God through whom the Messiah will come were destroyed because they were not faithful to God's covenant. This study will tell when the Jews will be ready for their Messiah.

Gabriel's report to Daniel was fulfilled as he had said: sixty-nine weeks of years or 483 years total. (Adding 450 years in BC plus 70 years in AD contains the 483 years.)

Some want to start the 483 years with the decree from King Cyrus to rebuild the temple to Ezra in 536 BC, but Ezra did not rebuild the walls and streets. Nehemiah rebuilt the walls and streets and set up the gate of Jerusalem.

During the Persian Empire, while King Artaxerxes I was reigning, Nehemiah was commissioned to rebuild the streets, walls, and gates of Jerusalem (Nehemiah 2). The year was about 450 BC. This commission started the clock on the 69 weeks of years or 483 years until the people of God were removed or cut off from their land.

Gabriel even tells of the destruction of Jerusalem and the temple. The people of the prince are Rome and its army. Daniel

---

21 Hull, *The Wall Chart of World History*

says they came in like a flood. This event happened in AD 70. The Roman Empire destroyed the temple and Jerusalem. All the Jews were scattered. For about 1,878[22] years, the Jews dreamed of going back to their homeland.

It makes one wonder if the people of Israel believed God would never destroy His temple. They may have thought they could live any way they wanted, and God would protect His temple. This shows us that God's covenant must be read, studied, and obeyed for God's protection.

The first time period of this prophecy has been fulfilled. History has recorded the information just as it was told to Daniel. The second time period is still future for us.

Second Time Period:
Seventieth Week of Daniel—Future

After World War II, the Jews started returning home in large numbers and in troubled times. They reestablished the nation of Israel on May 14, 1948. This had to happen for the King of Deceit to make a covenant of seven years with Israel during the seventieth week of Daniel, an event which is yet to be fulfilled. God even helped the Jews to reestablish their Hebrew language. This was nothing short of a miracle.

The second period starts with the King of Deceit making a seven-year covenant or treaty with the nation of Israel. It appears that the ten rulers of the last Gentile Empire, or the ten toes of iron and clay from the image in Daniel 2, will accept this King of Deceit as a king or leader in Europe of a new government which is likely to be called the "European Empire."

In Daniel 7:8, 20, the King of Deceit is the man Daniel sees as one horn that rises and uproots three of the original horns. In Daniel 8:9, he is the little horn that will become very great. In verse 23, he is the king who will rise from a group of people full of transgressors. The evil group of people are from the area of the Greek Empire

---

22 Israel became a nation in 1948, and Jerusalem was destroyed in AD 70 (1,948 − 70 = 1,878 years).

In Daniel 2, with the dream interpretation, Daniel does not mention the King of Deceit or that he is supported by a group of wicked people. God gives Daniel this information in visions that helps us see details about the King of Deceit: "Then he shall confirm a covenant with many for one week" (Daniel 9:27).

This time period is a week of seven years. For this writing, we will call these last seven years of the 490 years, or the last week of the "seventy weeks' prophecy," the *"seventieth week"* of Daniel. The first sixty-nine weeks of years have been fulfilled as was reviewed ending in AD 70, and the seventieth week of seventy weeks is still in the future. (See Table 2 near the end of this chapter.)

The King of Deceit, as the leader of a last Gentile world government, will make a covenant or treaty of seven years (one week) with the nation of Israel. This covenant or treaty will bring peace in the Middle East.

"Covenant with many" indicates how he will strengthen his dominance over the world. This will include Arab nations with whom he will make covenants as well. As the King of Deceit, he will deceive Israel and the Arab nations.

With the treaty, the King of Deceit may give Israel political covering to build their temple and reestablish their sacrifices and offerings. Haggai tells us in 2:9, "'The glory of this latter temple shall be greater than the former,' says the LORD of hosts." The nation of Israel will be excited to once again be able to worship the Lord with the Mosaic laws and ordinances.

For the first three and a half years, the King of Deceit will be at peace with Israel. During this time, he will increase his power and influence around the world.

Middle of the Week

After the King of Deceit has built his power base and system, he will turn against Israel for the last three and a half years of the seventieth week.

But in the middle of the week he shall bring an
end to sacrifice and offering. And on the wing of
abominations shall be one who makes desolate, even
until the consummation, which is determined, is
poured out on the desolate. (Daniel 9:27)

In the middle of the seventieth week, the King of Deceit will
end the sacrifices and offerings that have been reestablished in
Israel. This worship will be in the temple that has been built
during the peace brought by the seven-year treaty. (See Table 1
near the end of this chapter.)

The abomination will be in the temple where he will more
than likely set up something of himself to be worshiped. Thus,
he will stop the true worship of Almighty God.

And he said to me, "For two thousand three hundred
days; then the sanctuary shall be cleansed." (Daniel
8:14)

The sanctuary or temple must be rebuilt for this prophecy
to be fulfilled, for the Messiah to cleanse the temple when He
comes to this earth. (Table 1, "Building of the Temple.")

When the King of Deceit sets up an abomination in the wing
of the temple, Israel will realize he is not the Messiah. The
King of Deceit will turn on Israel.

God will protect the Jews in Israel. This is explained in the
next section, "Interpretation of Chapter 12."

In chapter 7, the King of Deceit speaks pompous words
against the Most High and oppresses the Jews. We are given
more information about him in Daniel 8:23–25. He will be
supported by people full of transgressions, a master of sinister
schemes, cause deceit to prosper, gain strength from evil
powers, cause devastation, destroy the mighty, destroy holy
people, exalt himself, and rise against the Prince of princes. The
Messiah will be the Prince of peace when He comes. The King
of Deceit will oppose the Messiah when He comes in the Day
of the Lord.

The phrase "until the consummation, which is determined, is poured out on the desolate" (Daniel 9:27) is fulfilled when the Ancient of Days destroys the King of Deceit (Daniel 7:26).

The book of Daniel, written more than 2,500 years ago, has given us much to understand about the King of Deceit and the evil that will come to rule this world. Remember, he comes from a group of people who are full of deceit and evil. He will have a charismatic personality, at first, and a large following.

The "seventieth week" is the last week of the seventy weeks of seven years. This fits into the time period of the ten toes on the image and the ten horns on the fourth beast which come up last. The ten horns on the fourth beast do not appear until the end of the iron influence which starts in the legs, goes down through the feet, and finally goes into the toes mixed with ceramic clay. Then one horn from the Greek Empire, the King of Deceit, will replace three of the original horns, rulers, and become mighty or in total control of the last Gentile government. He will rule the world for seven years.

The King of Deceit will have an army from the nations of the world. He will rule with an iron fist with all the latest knowledge known to humankind.

The latter days started when Israel became a nation about seventy-five years ago as of this writing. We are in the part of the foot near the ten toes kingdom. The last Gentile government to rule the world will soon develop and will be the seat of power for the King of Deceit. The European Union has been increasing their power base because the governing force is socialism. They cannot be voted out of office through a direct vote.

Interpretation of Daniel 11: Wrath from God

Daniel is strengthened to receive the vision by the likeness of a man from God (Daniel 10:18). The vision of chapter 8 is repeated in more detail in chapter 11. The vision describes the wars between the King of the North and the King of the South, the two dominant kings of the Greek Empire. History lets us know this prophecy was fulfilled as it was written. We will not take the time to review these events in history. Our focus is on the seventieth week of Daniel.

The two prominent kings of chapter 11 set up the global divide between the East and the West that has dominated the history of humankind ever since. This divide is seen in the image of chapter 2 with the two thighs and continues down the legs of the image into the feet. (See Figure 1.)

Several verses in chapter 11 prophecy of the King of Deceit. "Until the time of the end; because it is still for the appointed time" (Daniel 11:35). "Time of the end" lets us know that verses 36–39 are about the King of Deceit and his reign in the last Gentile government.

> Then the king shall do according to his own will: he shall exalt and magnify himself above every god, shall speak blasphemies against the God of gods, and shall prosper till the wrath has been accomplished; for what has been determined shall be done. (Daniel 11:36)

Daniel gives another glance at the King of Deceit toward the end of chapter 11. Additional facts are added to what we have already read about him. He will exalt and magnify himself while speaking unheard of things—blasphemies against the God who made the universe and against the coming Messiah.

The phrase "shall prosper till the wrath[23] has been accomplished" ties into the phrase in Daniel 8:19, "what shall happen in the latter time of the indignation." The same Hebrew transliterated word *za'am* is used in both phrases. In Daniel 11:36, it is translated "wrath," and in Daniel 8:19, it is translated "indignation." We have discussed the latter time earlier referring to the last Gentile government. Here the Hebrew word *za'am* refers to the end of the last Gentile government. *Za'am* is God's vehement wrath poured out on the world's armies in the Day of the Lord. This wrath of God falls

---

23 For the Hebrew translated word *za'am*, see Table 2.

on this ungodly world at the end of His judgments and wrath during the seventieth week[24] of Daniel.

The King of Deceit will be successful until the wrath of God is complete at the day of the Lord. God will pour out His wrath on the ungodly world and the King of Deceit and his armies at the end of His wrath on the world.

Then God will set up the kingdom of righteousness with the Messiah as the Ruler; the kingdom will never be destroyed (Daniel 2:44). Daniel is given this understanding thousands of years before it happens.

Interpretation of Daniel 12: Deliverance

> At that time Michael shall stand up, the great prince
> who stands watch over the sons of your people;
> and there shall be a time of trouble, such as never
> was since there was a nation, even to that time.
> (Daniel 12:1)

Israel's "time of trouble" will begin in the second half of the seventieth week of the seven-year treaty between Israel and the King of Deceit. At the start of the second half of the treaty, the King of Deceit will "set up an abomination that causes desolation" in the temple (Daniel 9:27, NIV). This is when the King of Deceit turns on Israel and tries to destroy them, a time of trouble "such as never was since there was a nation," in the middle of the seventieth week.

> At that time your people shall be delivered, everyone
> who is found written in the book (Daniel 12:1).

Daniel saw the deliverance of God's people, the Jews in Israel, when the trouble was worse than ever before in their history. Many ideas have been developed to explain how God will deliver His people, but God tells us in Zechariah chapter 12: "I will pour on the house of David and on the inhabitants

---

24 For seven years, the King of Deceit will rule the world through the last Gentile government.

of Jerusalem the Spirit of grace and supplication; then they will
look on Me whom they have pierced. Yes, they will mourn for
Him as one mourns for his only son, and grieve for Him as one
grieves for a firstborn" (Zechariah 12:10).

The Messiah will come down to the Mount of Olives
and reveal himself as the Messiah to all the Jews in Israel.
Israel as a nation will not draw back from Him as they did at
Mount Sinai. His presence will bring the grace that comes only
from our God. Israel as a nation pierced Him because they did
not accept the covenant God had given at Mont Sinai.

Those Jews who receive the Messiah as Lord at this time
will be allowed to flee into the Messiah's new Olivet Valley.

> And in that day His (the Messiah's) feet will stand on
> the Mount of Olives, which faces Jerusalem on the
> east. And the Mount of Olives shall be split in two,
> from east to west, making a very large valley; half of
> the mountain shall move toward the north and half
> of it toward the south. Then you shall flee through
> My mountain valley, for the mountain valley shall
> reach to Azal. Yes, you shall flee as you fled from
> the earthquake in the days of Uzziah king of Judah.
> (Zechariah 14:4–5)

What a wonderful protection from the King of Deceit and
his armies, for Israel to flee into the new Valley of Olivet. Many
Jews from Jerusalem and around it will flee to this new valley
created by their Messiah. They will be protected by the Messiah
for the entire 1,335 days. The safest place for any Jew on earth
will be in this new valley. This is why God is calling all Jews to
their homeland. Any Jew who is not in Israel will not be able to
enter the Valley of Olivet.

This event follows the Messiah being revealed to the
Jews in Israel. Both prophecies will be fulfilled, just as the
prophecies in the book of Daniel have been fulfilled up to
these events. Don't you want to be there?

The Jews outside the Jerusalem area but in Israel who are unable to get to the new Valley of Olivet will be protected where they take refuge. This will become clearer in the last chapter.

Daniel asked the man clothed in linen, "How long shall the fulfillment of these wonders be?" (12:6). Daniel was answered: "It shall be for a time, times, and half a time; and when the power of the holy people has been completely shattered, all these things shall be finished" (Daniel 12:7).

This time period is the first half of the seventieth week. The Jews are completely shattered when the King of Deceit sets up the abomination of desolation in the temple and stops their worship.

Daniel asked the man clothed in linen, "My lord, what shall be the end of these things?" (12:8).

> And from the time that the daily sacrifice is taken away, and the abomination of desolation is set up, there shall be one thousand two hundred and ninety days. Blessed is he who waits, and comes to the one thousand three hundred and thirty-five days. (Daniel 12:11–12)

In chapter 12, Daniel is given the time frame for the seventieth week of seven years. Daniel is given the divisions of the seven-year treaty which are the first and second halves.

The first half starts with the treaty between Israel and the King of Deceit and ends when worship in the temple is stopped which is 1,290 days or time, times and half a time (Daniel 7:25; 12:7). With thirty days a month, this would make it three and a half years.

The second half of the seventieth week of Daniel begins with the "abomination of desolation" by the King of Deceit to the end of the seven years, which is 1,335 days (see verse 12). These days are a little more than three and a half years based on thirty-day months.

The King of Deceit will demonstrate just who he is by setting up the abomination that causes desolation. This event takes place in the middle of the seventieth week of Daniel (9:27). By this evil act, he will turn on Israel to destroy them because they will know he is not the Messiah.

At this time the new valley is created by the Messiah to protect Israel. He will prove to Israel that He is the Messiah and fulfill many prophecies. Daniel calls this the "time of trouble" (12:1). Jeremiah calls it the "time of Jacob's trouble" (30:7).

During this time, the King of Deceit will wage war against the Jews outside of Israel and defeat them (Daniel 7:21). The Jews who are not in Israel do not receive the Messiah's protection of the new Olivet Valley because they not in the Promised Land.

It is certain that the King of Deceit will be destroyed at the end of the seven-year treaty, along with the last Gentile government the Ancient of Days—will pronounce judgment against the King of Deceit and destroy him and his armies of the world (Daniel 7:22, 26; 9:27).

Table 1: Building of the Temple

Seventieth Week
Reign of the King of Deceit

Starts with Seven-Year Treaty between Israel and Little Horn	End-Times 7-Year Treaty	End of Treaty
Israel Has Peace	Worship Stopped (Dan. 9:27) 2,300 Days . . (Dan. 8:14)	War with Jews Outside of Israel (Dan. 7:21) **Second Half** Temple Cleansed Israel Protected (Zek. 14:4-5)
Temple Built 230 Days **First Half**		
(Deduction)	1,209 Days (Dan. 12:11)	Abomination	1,335 Days (Dan. 12:12)
	Total 2,625 Days	Little Horn Destroyed

3 (5) (6)

Table 2: Book of Daniel

CHAPTERS

2 (Image)	Head	2 Arms / Chest	Belly / Thighs	Legs
	Gold	Silver	Bronze	Iron
	Babylon	Medes-Persia	Greece	Roman Empire
	vv. 32, 38	vv. 32, 39	vv. 32, 39	vv. 33, 41

7 (4 Beast)	Lion	Bear	Leopard	Dreadful
	With Wings	3 Ribs	4 Wings	Terrible
		In Mouth	4 Heads	Iron Teeth
	vv. 4, 17	vv. 5, 17	vv. 6, 17	vv. 7, 19–20, 23–24

8 (Ram / Goat)		Ram	Male Goat	
		With 2 Horns	1 Horn Replaced	
		1 Horn Higher	By 4 Horns	
		v. 3–7, 20	v. 5–8, 21, 22	

9
(70 Weeks
Of 7 Years)

Total 69 weeks = 483 years
7 weeks x 7 years = 49 years
69 weeks x 7 years = 434 years
─── vv. 24–26 ───
483 Years completed

450 BC
Nehemiah Rebuilds
Walls and Streets of Jerusalem
─── v. 25 ───

70 AD
Jerusalem
Destroyed
v. 26

11
(2 Kings)

King of North
King of South
2 Generals of Greece
vv. 5–30

12
(End Times)

─────

"Daniel, shut up the words, and seal the book until the time of the end." (Daniel 12:4)

Table 2: Book of Daniel
(Continued)

CHAPTERS				END-TIMES
2 (Image)	**Feet** Iron and Baked Clay vv. 33, 41	**10 Toes** Iron and Baked Clay vv. 41–42	**(Seventieth Week)** (Reign of King of Deceit) (Seven Years) 9:27	**Stone** God's Kingdom Never Destroyed vv. 34–35, 44–45
7 (4 Beast)		10 Horns 1 Horn Replaces 3 Horns vv. 7–8, 20–21, 24–25	Little Horn War with Jews 3½ Years vv. 8, 20–21, 25	Ancient of Days Seated Beast Slain vv. 9, 14, 22	Most High Kingdom vv. 18, 27
8 (Ram / Goat)		One Horn King of Deceit Rises from Wicked Base vv. 23–25		Latter Time Time of Indignation (za'am) v. 19	Rise against Prince-Messiah King of Deceit Broken by God v. 25
	Latter Days Israel a Nation May 14, 1948		**70th Week** Temple 1 week = 7 years Little Horn Makes Covenant With Israel 7 Years v. 27		
9 (70 Weeks of 7 Years)		Israel 7 Years Treaty with King of Deceit v. 27		Abomination Middle of Week v. 27	Consummation Poured Out on Him v. 27
11 (2 Kings)		King of Deceit Magnifies Himself v. 36–39		God's Wrath on King of Deceit v. 36	God's Wrath Is Complete v. 36
12 (End-Times)			1,290 Days	1,335 Days Time of Trouble For Israel v. 1	

Abomination

Name in Book
Delivered (New Valley)[38]
                                                                                                    Resurrection
v. 11 ___ v. 1, 11 __7, 12 ___ v. 2 ____9

---

[38]New Olivet Valley (Zechariah 14:4–5)

A Summary of the Prophecies of Daniel

Table 2 is an overview of the book of Daniel. Each row is an outline of a chapter in Daniel. The headings of the columns match the parts of the image in Nebuchadnezzar's dream (Daniel 2) and as laid out in Figure 1. This table provides an understanding that can be used to interpret other prophecies. This is the foundation for understanding God's plan till the end of time as we know it.

Column 1. The head represented the Babylonian Empire. Daniel tells King Nebuchadnezzar that he is the head of gold. In chapter 7, the general is depicted as a lion with wings. Nebuchadnezzar conquered the kingdoms of the known world. He was the first Gentile ruler of the world. God used Nebuchadnezzar's dream to reveal the empires that would follow his kingdom until the Messiah sets up His kingdom forever.

Column 2. The two arms and chest represented the kingdom of the Medes and Persians. The arms and chest of the image are made of silver. In chapter 7, the kings are depicted as a bear that captures all three regions of the known world at that time. The three ribs in the mouth of the bear depict the regions. The Medes and Persians are depicted as two horns on a ram in chapter 8. One horn grows higher and becomes dominant—the Persian kingdom.

During the Persian Empire, while King Artaxerxes I was reigning, Nehemiah was commissioned to rebuild the streets, walls, and gates of Jerusalem. This is recorded in Nehemiah's book. The year was about 450 BC. The commission started the clock on the sixty-nine weeks or 483 years until Jerusalem was destroyed in AD 70. The prophecy of the 483 years ended around the time Jerusalem was destroyed. Each chapter of Daniel gives details that help explain the total plan of God.

Column 3. The belly and thighs were the Greek Empire. The belly and thighs are made of bronze in the image. In

Daniel 7, the Greek Empire is depicted as a leopard with four wings and four heads. Alexander the Great moved swiftly as if he had four wings. When he died at the age of thirty-three, the four heads of the leopard represented the four prominent generals who divided the kingdom.

In chapter 8, Greece is depicted as a male goat with one broken horn. Four horns take the place of the broken horn, but not with the same power. Alexander the Great is represented by the one horn. The four horns on the male goat in chapter 8 are the same as the four heads on the leopard in chapter 7.

Out of the four generals, two became dominant. The end result was two centers of power: the East and the West, also known in Daniel 11 as the King of the North and the King of the South. They are represented by the thighs of the image (see Figure 1). We have discussed each of these points earlier, but now we are looking down the columns of Table 2.

Column 4. The legs of the image represented the Roman Empire and are made of iron. They represent the East and the West that became prominent during the Greek Empire. In chapter 7, the fourth beast represented the Roman Empire. It is depicted as a beast that Daniel could not describe as being like any other animal. He described it, instead, as a dreadful and terrible beast. It had iron teeth that it used to devour the whole earth, and it used its feet to trample the remains.

The influence of the Roman government is seen throughout the world even today. It was not destroyed by another power taking it over; instead, the Roman Empire fell apart into individual nations and regional powers. That is why we see the iron continuing into the rest of the image. However, in the feet it is mingled with ceramic clay. This depicts the nations of the earth even into the present time.

Column 5. In the fifth column, the feet of the image consists of iron and ceramic clay. Daniel tells us the kingdoms will be divided in that the people will not mix. They will have some of the strength of iron in them. The division of the East and the West are still represented by the two feet. Nothing is brought out in the following chapters about the feet. In Table 2, nothing is listed in that column from the chapters of Daniel.

Israel became a nation in 1948 which lets us know we are in the latter days. This event is inserted in the row for chapter 9 on Table 2. This places our time in the foot moving toward the ten toes which represents the last Gentile Empire that is soon to appear. Israel had to become a nation in order to make a treaty with the King of Deceit for the last seven years or the seventieth week of Daniel.

Column 6. The ten toes of the image are made of ceramic clay and iron. The Roman Empire was the last world government and is represented by the legs of iron. The iron from the legs extends down through the feet and into the toes. This fact gives us strong indication that the last Gentile government will be in Europe as a revised Roman Empire. This last Gentile European government will be led by ten leaders or super leaders who will dominate the world. In the book of Daniel, the emphasis is on the toes which are made of the same material as the feet.

Up to this point, our study has been confirmed by history, but the ten toes are still in our future. There are ten toes with five toes on each foot. Daniel says the nations will not mix just as iron and clay do not mix. They will not remain united any more than iron mixes with clay. We have seen this same development in countries around the world today where people do not mix.

Out of the feet ten kings will come to power in a revised European government representing the fourth beast. This new European Empire may develop from the current European Union which started March 25, 1957, with the Treaty of Rome and over time became the European Union. Most people do not realize the impact the Roman Catholic Church has on the European Union today.

In Daniel 7, the fourth beast was dreadful and terrible and had ten horns. These are the same as the ten toes of the image. The ten toes and ten horns represent ten kings or rulers who will come out of the feet. They will reestablish the Roman Empire as the last Gentile world government or a new European Empire from the basis or area of the last two empires which were European. They will have influence economically, politically, and militarily around the world.

When the new European Empire achieves this point, the King of Deceit (little horn) will arise and replace three of the original kings. We refer to him as the King of Deceit because that is how he gets into power. He will use deceptions the world has never seen before because the devil will be helping him.

The King of Deceit will make a seven-year treaty of peace with Israel and many nations. The remaining seven kings or rulers of the new European Empire will give their power to the King of Deceit.

Daniel 8 has more information about this time period. One horn rises out of rebels' reign or a people full of transgressions who have become completely wicked. The King of Deceit will come from the government of the male goat: the Greek Empire. They will be against anything related to God and hate anyone who believes in Him. This King of Deceit is the one in Daniel 7 who replaces three kings. He will be destroyed at the end of the seventieth week in the time of indignation of God's wrath.

In Daniel 9, the King of Deceit makes a treaty with Israel for seven years. This seven-year treaty starts the *seventieth week* of Daniel. It will give Israel the political cover to build the third temple. It has to be built for the King of Deceit to stop the worship with the Mosaic law.

In the middle of the treaty, the King of Deceit will set up the abomination in the temple. He will send his army against Israel but the Messiah will create a valley to protect them. Then he will make war with Jews around the world for three and a half years or 1,335 days.

In Daniel 11, the King of Deceit will magnify himself above every god. He will be successful until the time of wrath is completed.

Column 7. This is the time of the seventieth week of seven years, the period between the feet and the stone. We have titled this period the "Seventieth Week" of Daniel because there is no part of the image to use, but it fits.

In Daniel 7, the horn or King of Deceit will use the first half of the seventieth week to gain power worldwide. This is not stated in Scripture but is understood by many because it will take time to establish treaties with the nations of the world for a worldwide system.

In the second half of the seventieth week, the King of Deceit will make war against Jews around the world. He will speak boastfully or arrogantly. At the end of the seventieth week, God will take His seat, judge the King of Deceit, and destroy him.

In Daniel 8, the King of Deceit will rise "who understands sinister schemes" (v. 23). His power will not be his own, and he will destroy many and exalt himself above all. He will try to stop the Prince of princes, the Messiah, from setting up God's kingdom in Jerusalem. The King of Deceit's reign will last for seven years. At the end of this last Gentile government, he will face God's "indignation" (v. 19) or the Day of the Lord and be destroyed. God will destroy the King of Deceit and his armies.

Daniel 9 tells us that in the middle of the treaty of seven years, the King of Deceit will cause sacrifices and offerings to stop in the Jewish temple. He will set up an abomination that causes desolation in the temple in Jerusalem. Then all of Israel will know he is an impostor and not the Messiah. At this point, the King of Deceit will want to make war with Israel, but God will protect Israel as we saw in Zechariah's prophecies.

The wrath of God is brought up again in chapters 9 and 11 at the end of the seventieth week. God's judgments and wrath are against this ungodly world. The King of Deceit will be successful until the time of wrath and consummation is poured out on him which is completed in the Day of our Lord.

In Daniel 12, the abomination of the King of Deceit is recorded again. This time, Daniel is given the number of days for each time period. The daily sacrifice will be set up around the time that the treaty or covenant is made to bring peace to Israel. The King of Deceit will use this time to build his power system around the world. Then after 1,290 days, or three and a half years, the sacrifices will be abolished, and the King of Deceit will set up the abomination that causes desolation.

The great prince of God's realm, Michael, will stand watch over the Jewish people of God (12:1). When the little horn or King of Deceit turns to destroy the nation of Israel in the middle of the seventieth week, God provides deliverance. Everyone whose name is found written in the book (Life) will be delivered in the land of Israel.

This deliverance is recorded in Zechariah 14:4–5. When the feet of the Messiah touch the Mount of Olives, it will split and make a great valley that the Jews will be able to flee into, and God will protect them.

Daniel is told in 12:12, "Blessed is he who waits, and comes to the one thousand three hundred and thirty-five days." This period of 1,335 days will be the "time of trouble" such as never was since there was a nation of Israel (12:1).

Column 8. In the eighth column, the Stone that is cut out of the mountains without hands will smash the entire image of Daniel 2. The Stone will grind the image's materials to powder, and the wind will blow them away. The Stone, the Messiah, will set up a kingdom that will never be destroyed.

Daniel 7:13–14 tells us that God will give His people a kingdom that will last forever. The Messiah will be their King and reign forever.

Daniel 9:27 lets us know "the consummation, which is determined, is poured out on the desolate"—the King of Deceit will be destroyed.

When God's wrath is complete in chapter 11, the King of Deceit is included in the destruction.

The Messiah's reign will last forever. Then there will be the resurrection of the dead in Daniel 12:2.

Daniel served under several kings of Babylon—King Cyrus of the Persian Empire and King Darius of the Medes. It is clear that he never lost his relationship with the God of Israel. History lets us know he lived to be over the age of eighty. Anyone who serves God can and may be called to serve in the governments of this world. Daniel proved it.

In the last chapter, we will answer the question of why God is calling all Jews to their homeland.

Last Gentile World Government Rising

The latter days started when God allowed Israel to become a nation in one day as was pointed out earlier. This fact lets one know God is fulfilling the prophecies regarding Israel and the world. This includes Daniel's prophecies about the end-times.

The last Gentile government will be the ten toes government that the prophet Daniel records in his book. All the individual nations of the earth are depicted in Daniel as the feet of the image. The feet were made of iron and baked clay which shows that the nations and the people will not mix or agree.

From the feet of the image the last Gentile government will arise and be led by ten kings or super leaders. This government will be in Europe where the last two Gentile world empires were based—the Greek Empire and the Roman Empire.

The toes of the image are made of iron and baked clay like the feet. The iron from the legs, representing the Roman Empire will be the strength of these kings in the toes. They will set up a government that will influence and dominate the world when it is in full power under ten rulers. Some may call it a revised Roman Empire. For this writing, it will be called "European Empire" because there is no way to know what it will be called.

Because the nation of Israel is back in its own land, we know the time of the Gentile governments will be coming to an end because of Daniel's prophecies. Are there any political activities in Europe that would indicate the last Gentile government is developing? Since Israel has become a nation, is there any effort to bring about an empire in Europe? The answer is yes.

The Treaty of Rome was signed about nine years after Israel became independent by Belgium, France, Italy, Luxembourg, the Netherlands, and West Germany on March 25, 1957, and it came into force on January 1, 1958. Note where the treaty was signed by its name.

As a boy, I remember reading and hearing how the Pope was trying to get the countries of Europe to unite; otherwise, the United States of America would dominate the world for a long time. After many years of trying to get the leaders of the nations of Europe to agree on any treaty, this one was successful. The Treaty of Rome became known as the European Economic Community and became the foundation for future agreements.

The next major treaty was the Maastricht Treaty. The legal groundwork was laid for euro currency to be introduced on January 1, 1999. Currently, nineteen of the twenty-seven members of the European Union nations (eurozone) use the euro as their currency.

The last major treaty was the Treaty of Lisbon, signed December 13, 2007, and put into force on December 1, 2009. It amended the Treaty of Rome and the Maastricht Treaty by moving from requiring unanimity to requiring a qualified majority to pass decisions in many areas. The Treaty of Lisbon set up three permanent positions: president of the European Council, high representative of the Union for Foreign Affairs and Security Policy, and a Consolidated Legal Personality for the European Union. This started the federalization of the European Union.

The last position has not been filled as of this writing. They seem to be looking for a person to fill this position, and he will be able to determine his authority with the vague writing of this position. The hope is that he will be able to pull together all the loose ends. This is the ready-made position for the King of Deceit to step into power.

A religious order that has been present through all the planning and development processes to write the treaties has been the Pope and/or his leaders.

The European Union of nations is not a democracy; it is a socialist government that may be the beginning of the fulfillment of the prophecies of Daniel and other prophets. We will be able to watch and see when they become fully united or form an empire.

This developing world government in Europe is happening while God is fulfilling many prophecies. God is bringing many more Jews back to the Jewish homeland. The nations of the world are lining up with the alliances of nations as prophesied. The world is becoming more godless as the years pass.

European Union (EU) influence has been increasing because of their treaties with individual nations. Each treaty is for three to seven years as a rule. Each time a treaty is renewed by the EU, they increase their influence over that nation, by requiring that nation to increase their holding in the Euro currency for their reserve. No other country in the world requires such a treaty for their currency that the author has found.

In the past, and it may still be true, two countries are not included in the treaty portfolio of the EU—Japan and the United States of America. It seems the EU is doing its best to surpass these two nations.

6

Answers

1. HAS GOD KEPT HIS PROMISE TO BRING HIS PEOPLE OF ISRAEL BACK TO THEIR HOMELAND AFTER AD 70?

> It shall come to pass in that day that the Lord shall set His hand again the *second time* to recover the remnant of His people who are left, from Assyria and Egypt, from Pathros and Cush, from Elam and Shinar, from Hamath and the islands of the sea. He will set up a banner for the nations, and will assemble the outcasts of Israel, and gather together the dispersed of Judah from the four corners of the earth. (Isaiah 11:11–12, emphasis added by author)

The Jews came back from their Babylonian captivity around 536 BC. They were scattered out of their land in AD 70 when the Roman Empire destroyed Jerusalem and their temple. In the above verses, God is letting us know He will bring a remnant of the Jews back to their homeland again, which is termed a "second time." They will come from the whole earth.

> Now the LORD says, who formed Me from the womb to be His Servant, to bring Jacob back to Him, so that Israel is gathered to Him. (For I shall be glorious in the eyes of the LORD, and My God shall be My strength), indeed He says, "It is too small a thing that You should be My Servant to raise up the tribes of Jacob, and to restore the preserved ones of Israel; I will also give You as a light to the Gentiles, that You

should be My salvation to ends of the earth."
(Isaiah 49:5–6)

This promise is repeated in Isaiah 49:12. God promises to
bring the Jews back to their land from the ends of the earth.

The wilderness and the wasteland shall be glad for
them, and the desert shall rejoice and blossom as the
rose; it shall blossom abundantly and rejoice, even
with joy and singing. The glory of Lebanon shall be
given to it, the excellence of Carmel and Sharon. They
shall see the glory of the LORD, the excellency of our
God. (Isaiah 35:1–2)

This has come true since Jews started returning in great
numbers in the 1940s during and after the Second World War.

Who are these who fly like a cloud, and like doves to
their roosts? Surely the coastlands shall wait for Me;
and the ships of Tarshish will come first, to bring their
sons from afar, their silver and their gold with them, to
the name of the LORD your God, and to the Holy One
of Israel, because he has glorified you. (Isaiah 60:8–9)

Years ago, people could not understand the words "fly like
a cloud" but we now know they have returned on airplanes and
are still returning on airplanes. This prophecy is being fulfilled
in our generation: history records that they came on ships first.
They came with their belongings.

Thus says the Lord GOD: "Indeed I Myself will search
for My sheep and seek them out. As a shepherd seeks
out his flock on the day he is among his scattered
sheep, so will I seek out My sheep and deliver them
from all the places where they were scattered on a
cloudy and dark day. And I will bring them out from
the peoples and gather them from the countries, and
bring them to their own land; I will feed them on
the mountains of Israel, in the valleys and in all the
inhabited places of the country." (Ezekiel 34:11–13)

This promise is repeated in Ezekiel 36:8–11, 24 and 37:21. The terms "cloudy and dark" mean troubled times. God is seeking those who have not returned to their land of Israel. What will it take for those Jews to return? God is calling them.

> For the children of Israel shall abide many days without king or prince, without sacrifice or sacred pillar, without ephod or teraphim. Afterward the children of Israel shall return and seek the LORD their God and David their king. They shall fear the LORD and His goodness in the *latter days*. (Hosea 3:4–5, emphasis added by author)

The Israelites were out of their land for about 1,878[25] years, which fits the "many days." Scripture lets one know they will return in the "latter days" which fits with their returning and establishing the Nation of Israel in 1948. We have seen how the latter days recorded in Daniel's prophecy fits the Nation of Israel's timing in previous chapters.

> Who has heard such a thing? Who has seen such things? Shall the earth be made to give birth in one day? Or shall a nation be born at once? For as soon as Zion was in labor, she gave birth to her children. (Isaiah 66:8)

God is keeping His promise by bringing the Jews back to their homeland, a return which started during the Second World War. Yes! The nation of Israel was born in one day on May 14, 1948. Jews, who are God's special people, reestablished the Nation of Israel as prophesied. God is fulfilling other prophecies after this one.

God gave Israel control of the city of Jerusalem on June 7, 1967. This was nineteen years after they became a nation against over whelming odds. This proves that God is working with the nation of Israel as He promised. The prophecies about Israel in the latter days are being fulfilled. God even helped Israel to reestablish the Hebrew language.

1 Israel's independence was 1948 minus seventy years when Jerusalem was destroyed by the Roman Empire.

These Scriptures make it clear that the creation of the nation of Israel is by the strong arm of God working on their behalf. God has kept His promise to the children of Abraham. All the promises from Daniel and the other prophets will come true as surely as Israel was born in one day.

There is a reason God is establishing Israel again. Israel has to be in place for the other prophecies of the *latter days* to be fulfilled. Israel is a key to knowing we are in the latter days and heading into the end-times.

God has brought the Jews back to their own homeland using different methods of transportation, including ships and airplanes, as the prophecies recorded. He also reestablished their native language, Hebrew. God has given Israel control of Jerusalem. This is happening in our day. God is working with Israel to fulfill the end-times prophecies.

Who is like the Lord God who is full of mercy, keeps His promises, and lovingly cares for His people?

2. ARE THERE SIGNS THE LAST GENTILE WORLD EMPIRE IS DEVELOPING?

The nations of Europe were guided by the Pope and his leaders to form the Treaty of Rome between Belgium, France, Italy, Luxembourg, the Netherlands, and West Germany on March 25,1957. It was put into force on January 1, 1958. This was about ten years after Israel became a nation, independent and free.

The next major treaty was the Maastricht Treaty. The legal groundwork was laid for euro currency to be introduced on January 1, 1999. Currently nineteen of the twenty-seven members of the European Union nations (called the eurozone) use the euro as their currency.

The last major treaty was the Treaty of Lisbon, signed December 13, 2007, and put into force December 1, 2009. It amended the Treaty of Rome and the Maastricht Treaty. It moved from requiring unanimity to requiring a qualified majority to pass decisions in many areas. This treaty set up three permanent positions: President of the European Council, High Representative of the Union for Foreign Affairs and Security Policy, and a Consolidated Legal Personality for the European Union. This treaty started the federalization of the European Union.

The last position set up by the Treaty of Lisbon has not been filled as of this writing. They seem to be looking for a person to fill this position, and he will be able to determine his authority with the vague writing of his position. There is hope he will be able to pull together all the loose ends. This is a ready-made position for the King of Deceit to step into power.

This European Union of nations is not a democracy; it is a socialist government that may be the beginning of the fulfillment of the prophecies of Daniel. We will be able to watch and see when they become fully united or form an empire.

When the European Union or European Empire is ruled by ten rulers or super leaders, one will know it is the fulfillment of Daniel's prophecy given by Gabriel (Daniel 8:16–19).

Then the little horn (Daniel 7:8; 8:9) or other horn (7:20) or a king (8:23) or he (9:27) will rise and make a treaty or covenant with Israel for seven years which is called the "seventieth week" of Daniel. This ruler is the King of Deceit. This treaty or covenant will give Israel political cover to build their third temple. The Jews will establish the worship to their God in their temple with the Mosaic sacrifices.

Daniel is told that this first half of the seven years treaty is 1,260 days or three and one-half years (Daniel 7:25; 12:7, 11).

3. WHAT DOES GOD DO FOR THE JEWS IN THE MIDDLE OF THE SEVENTIETH WEEK?

In the middle of the seventieth week of Daniel, the King of Deceit will set up the abomination that leads to desolation in the Jewish temple in Jerusalem. This action by the king will let all Jews know he is not for them but against them. As a nation, the Jews will turn against the King of Deceit. The King will turn on them to kill them, but the Messiah will protect them (Daniel 12:1).

The Messiah will do two things at this time:

A. The Messiah will reveal himself as the promised one from God on the Mount of Olivet.

This is the main reason God is calling all Jews to their homeland.

The Messiah will stand on the Mount of Olivet. He will reveal himself to the nation of Israel as their promised Messiah:

> And I will pour on the house of David and on the inhabitants of Jerusalem the Spirit of grace and supplication; then they will *look on Me* whom they pierced. Yes, they will mourn for Him as one mourns for his only son, and grieve for Him as one grieves for a firstborn. (Zechariah 12:10, emphasis added by author)

The Jews, as a nation, have pierced their God's heart by not reading and obeying the covenant He offered them on Mount Sinai as recorded in the book Exodus and the first chapter of this book. We have reviewed how the people turned their backs on God during the time of the judges. It seems each generation rebelled against the Lord God, so He sent judges to guide them.

The people of the northern kingdom, Israel, never had a king who fully trusted in God. Their hearts were far from God. They rejected the prophets who brought them God's word. The prophets' call for the people to return to God and obey Him were laughed at and some prophets were even killed.

People of the southern kingdom, Judah, only had a few kings who loved God's law and obeyed His commandments like their father King David. Our study shows how they worshiped idols instead of the God of Israel. It appears the final action by both kingdoms that caused God's wrath to fall on them was when they sacrificed their sons and daughters to idol gods. When Israel came back from Babylon after seventy years of captivity, they created their own ordinances and followed them instead of the law of the covenant.

It seems Jews around the world will not see their Messiah on the Mount of Olivet. The reason for believing this is they will not be protected by the Messiah against the King of Deceit's army. (Daniel 7:21, 25).

B. The Messiah will protect the Jews in their homeland.

> And in that day His feet will stand on the Mount of Olives, which faces Jerusalem on the east. And the Mount of Olives shall be split in two, from east to west, making a very large valley; half of the mountain shall move toward the north and half of it toward the south. Then you shall flee through My mountain valley, for the mountain valley shall reach to Azal. Yes, you shall flee as you fled from the earthquake in the days of Uzziah king of Judah. (Zechariah 14:4–5)

The last half of the seventieth week of Daniel, the Messiah will protect the Jews who accept Him as Lord in the land of Israel. This protection will last for the 1,335 days which is the end-time of the reign of the King of Deceit.

The only Jews who will be protected are the ones in Israel who have accepted the Messiah as Lord. The evil one will drive the King of Deceit to destroy every Jew.

God is calling all Jews to their homeland where He will protect them.

The new Olivet Valley created by the Messiah is a prophecy that fits into the book of Daniel because it happens during the time of trouble for Israel: "Such as never was since there was a nation, even to that time" (Daniel 12:1).

God's call for all Jews to come home is like when He called Abraham. To obey will give each Jew the opportunity to experience these promises.

As Amos said years ago, "Seek the LORD and live" (Amos 5:6). Seeking the Lord requires obedience. Do not get hung up on the person delivering the message; instead, study God's word yourself and obey God.

In the second half of the seventieth week, God will pour out His judgments and wrath on the whole world. The Jews in the new Valley of Olivet will be protected as they were in Egypt. These are not made-up words; they will come true as God has promised.

Daniel is told this period is called a "time of trouble" for the Jews in Israel but the Messiah will protect them in His new Valley of Olivet. Also, for those who cannot get to the valley He will protect them where they hide. "Come, my people, enter your chambers, and shut your doors behind you; hide yourself, as it were, for a little moment, until the indignation is past" (Isaiah 26:20).

The word "indignation" is the Hebrew translated word *za'am* which is God's fury poured out on the armies of the King of Deceit at the end of his reign of seven years. The same word is used in Daniel 8:19 which states: "The indignation; for at the appointed time the end shall be." When God's indignation is poured out, God will protect the Jews who have accepted Him but could not get to the Olivet Valley.

The same Hebrew word is translated "wrath" in Daniel 11:36. The King of Deceit "shall prosper till the wrath (*za'am*) has been accomplished; for what has been determined shall be done." When the Hebrew *za'am* is used, most often it is referring to the indignation during the Day of the Lord.

4. WHEN IS THE DAY OF THE LORD?

To help one to understand the prophecies of Daniel, this study looks at the Scriptures related to the Day of the Lord. The best word to follow on this subject is God's "indignation"—the transliterated Hebrew word *za'am*.

Za'am is used twenty-two times and is the word to review in Scripture in relation to the Day of the Lord. It is translated into the New King James Version as "indignation" twenty times, "rage" one time, and "anger" one time. This study will look at the times it is used regarding God's wrath or indignation. It will be highlighted in each verse.

> But the LORD is the true God; He is the living God and the everlasting King. At His wrath the earth will tremble, and the nations will not be able to endure His *indignation*. (Jeremiah 10:10, emphasis added by author)

> "Therefore wait for Me," says the LORD, "until the day I rise up for plunder; My determination is to gather the nations to My assembly of kingdoms, to pour on them My *indignation*, all My fierce anger; all the earth shall be devoured with the fire of My jealousy. (Zephaniah 3:8, emphasis added by author)

God is the one who assembles the armies of the nations to pour out His indignation or His fury and wrath. Joel tells us that these armies will come up the Valley of Jehoshaphat or the Kidron Valley.

> God is jealous, and the LORD avenges; the LORD avenges and is furious. The LORD will take vengeance on His adversaries, and He reserves wrath for His enemies. . . . The mountains quake before Him, the hills melt, and the earth heaves at His presence, Yes, the world and all who dwell in it. Who can stand before His *indignation*? And who can endure the fierceness of His anger? His fury is poured out like fire, and the rocks are thrown down by Him. (Nahum 1:2, 5–6)

The timing of God's indignation and fierce wrath being poured out on the nations of this world is given in Daniel.

Gabriel (8:16) tells Daniel that "the vision refers to the time of the end" (8:17) The "time of the end" is not the end of the world but the end of the Gentile kingdoms or governments. The last Gentile government is the reign of the King of Deceit, so God's indignation is at the end of the seven-year treaty with Israel.

For this study, the little horn and the other horn are called the King of Deceit. At the end of the seven-year treaty he has with Israel, he will gather the armies of the world against Israel. The Messiah will be the one who pours out God's indignation on the armies of the King of Deceit in the Valley of Jehoshaphat.

> Then the king shall do according to his own will: he shall exalt and magnify himself above every god, shall speak blasphemies against the God of gods, and shall prosper till the wrath (*za'am*) has been accomplished; for what has been determined shall be done. (Daniel 11:36)

The words "till the wrath has been accomplished" refers to the same indignation recorded in Daniel 8:19. "The consummation, . . . is poured out" recorded in Daniel 9:27 is the same word and timing. God's "wrath (*za'am*—indignation) has been accomplished" is recorded in Daniel 11:36 and quoted above. Therefore, one can see when God's indignation is poured out on the armies and enemies of God. "I will also gather all nations, and bring them down to the Valley of Jehoshaphat; and I will enter into judgment with them there" (Joel 3:2).

This gathering by God brings the armies of the nations that follow the King of Deceit to the Kidron Valley or the valley of Jehoshaphat between Jerusalem and the Mount of Olivet. The King of Deceit thinks he the one who orchestrated the gathering of all his armies against Jerusalem but God is who initiated it.

Not only will God destroy the King of Deceit with His indignation but He will gather all the armies of the world and destroy them with His indignation. "Come near, you nations, to hear; and heed, you people! Let the earth hear, and all that is in it, the world and all things that come forth from it. For the *indignation* of the Lord is against all nations, and His fury against all their armies; He has utterly destroyed them, He has given them over to the slaughter" (Isaiah 34:1–2, emphasis added by author).

God's indignation will destroy the armies of the world. Not one will escape. "For it is the day of the LORD's vengeance, the year of recompense for the cause of Zion" (Isaiah 34:8).

Note: God's indignation is against the armies of the nations of the world who come against Israel. It may include their military home bases around the world as well. "You marched through the land in *indignation*; You trampled the nations in anger" (Habakkuk 3:12, emphasis added by author).

The Day of the Lord marks the time that God will take vengeance on the enemies of Israel. The timing has been made clear with this study.

5. HOW DOES THE MESSIAH PROTECT ISRAEL DURING THE INDIGNATION?

Some verses are repeated here to answer this question. Those Jews in Israel who are unable to get to the Olivet Valley are protected where they hide.

> Come, my people, enter your chambers, and shut your doors behind you; hide yourself, as it were, for a little moment, until the indignation is past. For behold, the LORD comes out of His place to punish the inhabitants of the earth for their iniquity; the earth will also disclose her blood, and will no more cover her stain. (Isaiah 26:20–21)

> When you see this, your heart shall rejoice, and your bones shall flourish like grass; the hand of the LORD shall be known to His servants, and His indignation to His enemies. For behold, the LORD will come with fire and with His chariots, like a whirlwind, to render His

anger with fury, and His rebuke with flames of fire.
(Isaiah 66:14–15)

Those Jews who have accepted the Messiah will rejoice
when they know their enemies have been destroyed. Their
Messiah will be victorious over all their enemies. It will be a
great time of rejoicing.

God says not to fear because He will save each believing
Jew. Do not fear going back to your Jewish homeland. The
Lord God is on your side as you trust Him. "Say to those who
are fearful-hearted, "Be strong, do not fear! Behold, your God
will come with vengeance, with the recompense of God; He
will come and save you" (Isaiah 35:4).

6. How Do I, As a Jew, Answer God's Call?

From your heart, accept the Lord God as your only and true
God. Put your trust, from your heart, in the Lord to lead, guide,
and protect you. Put faith in God's promises as Abraham did.

Hear, O Israel: The LORD our God, the LORD is one!
You shall love the LORD your God with all your heart,
with all your soul, and with all your strength. And
these words which I command you today shall be in
your heart (Deuteronomy 6:4–6).

Second, start or continue to read and study the Scriptures,
the words from our God. How will you be able to obey God's
covenant unless you know it?

Then go to the synagogue when the Scriptures are read and
studied. Also study them on your own, asking God to help you.

Finally, if you are not in your homeland, start planning to
move there to answer God's call to come home. Then you will
be able to see the Messiah when He comes to reveal himself to
all Israel.

You also can be protected by your Messiah when the King of Deceit turns on all Jews. You will be protected from God's indignation that will be poured out on the armies of the nations who are enemies of God.

God is calling you to serve Him only and come back to your homeland!

Printed in the United States
by Baker & Taylor Publisher Services